THE FIRST ENCOUNTER

Глубокоуважаемой и милой Нине Николаевне Берберовой с искренним расположением и дружбой

Андрей Белый. 22 года
Берлинъ
Бонн.

The First Encounter
by Andrey Bely

Translated and Introduced by Gerald Janeček

Preliminary Remarks, Notes, and Comments
by Nina Berberova

Princeton University Press
Princeton, New Jersey

Copyright © 1979 by Princeton University Press
Published by Princeton University Press, Princeton, New Jersey
In the United Kingdom: Princeton University Press, Guildford, Surrey

ALL RIGHTS RESERVED

Library of Congress Cataloging in Publication Data will be
found on the last printed page of this book

Publication of this book has been aided by a grant
from the Paul Mellon Fund of Princeton University Press

This book has been composed in VIP Bembo

Clothbound editions of Princeton University Press books
are printed on acid-free paper, and binding materials are
chosen for strength and durability

Printed in the United States of America by Princeton
University Press, Princeton, New Jersey

Frontis: Facsimile of Bely's inscription on Nina Berberova's copy of
Pervoe svidanie, Berlin, 6 October 1922

CONTENTS

vii   LIST OF ILLUSTRATIONS
ix   ACKNOWLEDGMENTS
xi   INTRODUCTION
xxiii   PRELIMINARY REMARKS
1   *THE FIRST ENCOUNTER*
91   NOTES AND COMMENTS ON THE POEM
131   APPENDIX I
133   APPENDIX II

LIST OF ILLUSTRATIONS

1. Map of Moscow, ca. 1912
2. Facsimile title page of the Alkonost edition, 1921
3. Facsimile title page of the Slovo edition, 1922

ACKNOWLEDGMENTS

We gratefully acknowledge Professors Simon Karlinsky and Robert Hughes, both of the Russian Department, University of California, Berkeley, for their invaluable and friendly help during our preparation of this book.

N. B.
G. J.

INTRODUCTION

I

When Bely's poetry is praised, *The First Encounter (Pervoe svidanie)* is given a place of special honor; when his poetry is denounced, the poem is typically named as the one exception. Of all this great writer's works, it remains the one whose artistic merit and value are unassailed. Some critics even place it among the finest achievements of twentieth-century Russian poetry.[1]

The poem is divided into four numbered, but untitled, parts and a Prologue and Epilogue. The Prologue is an introductory exhortation in which the poet commands his tongue (language) to revivify its powers for a flight of verbal wonder-working. Part 1 invokes the atmosphere of turn-of-the-century Moscow with its mixture of entrenched positivism and new spiritualistic trends. We see the poet as a university student who is both modish and yet serious as he tries to orient himself in the cultural variety and upheaval of the time. Part 2 describes Bely's relationship with the Solovyov family, including the famous philosopher Vladimir Solovyov. Part 3, the focal point of the work, describes in striking and extraordinary images a concert at the Noblemen's Assembly Hall and Bely's reaction to seeing the beautiful society lady, "Zariná," there. Part 4 takes place immediately after the concert and depicts the poet's return home and encounter with the spirit of Vladimir Solovyov on the way. The Epilogue evokes the mood of peace that results from reflecting on the events of twenty years before.

This verse memoir provides Bely the occasion for demonstrating brilliant poetic craftsmanship and seemingly effortless improvisation. Although the poem is, in many respects, not especially innovative compared with Bely's other works, and though it uses a traditional meter, yet

---

[1] S. Karlinsky, "Symphonic Structure in Andrej Belyj's 'Pervoe svidanie,' " *California Slavic Studies*, 6 (1971), 70; O. Ilinsky, "O poeme Andreya Belogo 'Pervoe svidanie,' " *Novy Zhurnal*, no. 90 (New York, 1968), pp. 98-111.

it is also free of unsuccessful groping and unrealized goals. It can thus be looked upon as Bely's most perfect artistic achievement.

The First Encounter can also be appreciated as a compendium of Bely's lifework in literature. In addition to being his best poem, it suggests his memoirs, since it deals with some of the same subject matter as *Na rubezhe dvukh stoletiy* and *Nachalo veka* (Moscow life of the time, V. Solovyov, the M. Solovyov family, university professors, Margarita Kirillovna Morozova ["Zarina"], and more), although the specific instance of the concert of Part 3 is not described in the memoirs. Bely's theories of language, as presented in several articles of his *Simvolizm* (1910) and in *Glossaloliya* (1922), are evident particularly in the Prologue with its reference to the theurgic power of language and of the tongue leaping high, the latter idea being illustrated literally in *Glossaloliya* with drawings of "tongue gestures." Of course, Bely's role as the leading proponent of Vladimir Solovyov's philosophy can be seen emerging, and a central place in *The First Encounter* is given to this relationship; lines 1291-95 indicate that the Encounter is as much with Solovyov as it is with Zarina; Part 4, in fact, suggests a passing of the mantle from the philosopher's shoulders to those of the poet. And Bely's theories of iambic tetrameter (elucidated in the Preliminary Remarks by Nina Berberova) are finely illustrated in the verse practice of the poem. One critic has even devoted attention to the fact that some of the techniques and orientation in the poem were the result of Bely's long course of experimentation in prose.[2] Finally, as is clear from the Notes and Commentary, the poem can be looked at as a referential survey of the best moments in the history of Russian iambic tetrameter, with the names of Lomonosov, Pushkin, Lermontov, and Blok figuring in the picture.

Perhaps only Bely's relationship with Rudolf Steiner and the anthroposophy movement is not as evident as might have been expected, considering that the poem was written before the official parting of ways between Bely and Steiner in October-December 1921. The few indirect references to things Steinerian are pointed out in the notes. Another indirect connection can be made via *Glossaloliya* and the discussion there of eurythmy, but no direct references to Bely's absorption with Steiner are explicit. Of course, the poem deals with a period before Bely knew about Steiner and before anthroposophy had even come into being as an offshoot of theosophy. Probably the flash of backward-looking creativity

[2] Ilinsky, ibid., p. 101-2.

was a poet's form of escape from the turmoil at hand, which was not unconnected with anthroposophy itself.

II

The division of labor for the present volume is as follows: Nina Berberova's primary responsibility is for the Notes and Commentary, mine is for the Introduction, the English translation, and the Appendices. However, our efforts have been truly collaborative: we have read, discussed, and criticized each other's contributions to such an extent that all parts of the book can be considered the product of both our labors. "Primary responsibility" should therefore be interpreted only as indicating the person who has had the last word.

My priorities for the English translation were: (1) literal accuracy, (2) observation of the iambic meter, (3) maintenance of word repetition, and (4) soundplay, rhymes, and so forth that could be introduced without detracting from the first three priorities. I believe I have succeeded (with considerable assistance from Nina Berberova) in achieving the first priority. The Notes and Commentary supplement the translation by giving nuances and connotations that do not come through in English, and they provide alternate translations. The second priority was also reasonably well achieved in that most of the lines are in acceptable iambs, though the number of feet varies to trimeter or pentameter fairly frequently. Lines opening with a downbeat (' ¯ ¯ ' ¯ ' . . .) are more frequent in the translation than in the original, but this practice is more natural in English with its inclination to stress initial syllables. There are also a few other rhythmic licenses, but none, it is hoped, so radical as to disrupt the rhythmic flow. For the third priority, every attempt was made to find translations of words and passages that would be suitable for all occurrences of that word or passage. This was achieved with few exceptions, and passage repetitions should be readily obvious in the translation. The fourth priority was a random affair. Basically, no attempt was made to seek out rhymes or reproduce the rhyme scheme in any way. The rhymes that do appear in the translation are either the gift of fortune or, often, the result of Bely's use of international words or Russian-English cognates. Whenever possible, such words were kept in rhyme position. The soundplay that is found in the translation usually does not correspond precisely to the original, but was introduced wherever alternative

INTRODUCTION

word choices allowed. However, when soundplay or wordplay was particularly important to the passage (e.g. lines 756-60, 807-8) an extra effort was made to reproduce it somehow. In many instances, Nina Berberova's notes have been able to salvage the situation by pointing out sonic aspects of the Russian text that cannot be found in the translation.

III

Structure

As is the case to varying degrees with most of Bely's artistic works from the early *Symphonies* on, *The First Encounter* employs passage repetition for structural purposes. The four-part arrangement and the high degree of such repetition easily suggest comparison with the *Symphonies*, and, in fact, a study of the "symphonic" structure of the poem has already been made.[3] However, such an analysis seems to be viable not on the basis of literal passage repetition as one would expect, but only on the basis of "complexes of ideas," which are hard to define precisely and delimit properly so they can be easily identified. A structure of this sort would not, in any case, be evident to most readers.

But the existence of patterns (however unclear) of passage repetition will be obvious to any attentive reader. Typically there is a single reiteration of a passage, often with some slight changes. These reiterations tend to create the impression of a circular arrangement within a part, but do not form a neat prograde or retrograde pattern (see Appendix I). Such repetition is a minor matter in Part 1, is most regular in Part 2, and reaches a highpoint of elaborateness in Part 3. Each of these parts has, in addition, a single instance of a double reiteration (1: lines 49, 131, 221; 2: lines 299-302, 412-15, 685-88; 3: lines 820-27, 984-86, 1080-87). In Part 1, these passages are almost equally spaced, in Part 2 the second occurrence is off center toward the front, and in Part 3 the second and third occurrences are pushed to the rear of the part. Evidently Bely was not as interested here in a precise spacing of the reiterations as he was in *Kotik Letaev*, his novel written in 1915-16.

While Part 4 is similar to Part 1 in having only a pair of passage repetitions belonging exclusively to itself, it is characterized by the reiteration of much material from the earlier parts (chiefly Part 2, but also 3; not Part

---

[3] Karlinsky, op. cit.

INTRODUCTION

1, however⁴). Moreover, there are in Part 3 reiterations of several passages from Part 2.

If one were therefore to describe the structure of *The First Encounter* on the basis of passage repetition, one would say that it is a structure of accumulated correspondences. However, perhaps due to the relative shortness of the work, such a structure is not as developed or complex as that in *Kotik Letaev* or *Petersburg*. One should not, of course, neglect to add to the full picture the repetition of smaller-than-line-sized units of text such as words and individual images. The total impression is of a rich, irregularly patterned tapestry with a unity of tone, but without a rigid structure.

Rhythm

In consonance with Bely's theories, the poem is characterized by great rhythmic variety. In his terms, this means a high frequency of pyrrhic feet and a low incidence of lines with all four stresses. A thorough study of this has already been made by K. Taranovsky and his results are used here as a statistical basis for additional commentary.⁵ The types of rhythmic variations are:

I	-/	-/	-/	-/
II	--	-/	-/	-/
III	-/	--	-/	-/
IV	-/	-/	--	-/
V	-/	--	--	-/
VI	--	-/	--	-/

The high frequency of rhythmic variation VI is characteristic of the poem. Taranovsky notes that such "paeonic" (as Bely would call them) lines are especially evident in exalted moments of pathos. These lines tend to be composed of a long adjective and a shorter noun. Examples:

>   1007   S neimenuemoyu siloy
>   S neizrechennykh alliluy

---

⁴ This fact is peculiar in the context of symphonic structure, if it is applicable here, since symphonies which reiterate material from earlier movements in the last movement almost always draw this material from the *first* movement, thus creating a circular structure.

⁵ K. F. Taranovsky, "Chetyryokhstopny yamb Andreya Belogo," *International Journal of Slavic Linguistics and Poetics*, 10 (1966), 127-47. For his figures for the poem, see Appendix II (for comparison, Taranovsky's figures for Pushkin's "Medny vsadnik" have been included).

1024 Katastroficheskoy tsevnitsy
I miloglazaya lazur',
I potseluynaya dennitsa:

1045 Neumolyaemoy alchby—
Nerazryvnye migolyoty
Neotrazhaemoy sud'by . . .

The fact that such adjectives are often negative has led Eikhenbaum[6] to see in this a continuation of the tradition of Lermontov's *Demon*, which has such lines as "Nevyrazimoe smyaten'e" and "Neotrazimoyu mechtoy."[7] No doubt a detailed comparative study of these two poems would be interesting and fruitful. No doubt also, the evocation of Lermontov by Bely is not accidental.

Taranovsky's observation that lines of rhythmic variation VI are usually grouped at emotional peaks, and also an awareness of Bely's interest in rhythmic "figures" led me to study the poem for possible rhythmic patterns of several lines or more in length. However, the picture appears to be much the same as that for structure; namely, there are individual patterns to be noted, small groupings of lines of similar rhythm, but no larger, strictly observed pattern that is evident. Flexibility and improvisation seem to be the key qualities of the poem in all areas.

Rhythm is made to go hand in hand with other elements to underline concepts or create contrasts. An example would best serve to explain how Bely does this. The pattern of rhythmic variations in lines 170-82 is: IV, V, II, IV, II, I, IV, VI, VI, IV, I, VI. The passage opens with lines of types IV and V to which the next line (of type II) is in distinct contrast. This line introduces the poet's father, whose positivistic mathematical mind cannot understand his son's divagations. The rhythmic dissonance is even more evident in the direct quotation attributed to him (lines 174-75), which consists of: (1) again a type II variation, but with a half-stress on the first syllable, which disrupts the rhythm slightly and reads a bit awkwardly, and (2) a type I of regular iambic with no pyrrhics. A thematic interpretation of this passage based on rhythm might go as follows: Dean "Letaev" has a tin ear for poetic rhythm (line 174) and what he does appreciate and understand is very rigid and "mathematical" (line 175).

---

[6] Boris M. Eikhenbaum, *Lermontov* (Leningrad, 1924; Fink reprint, 1967), p. 163, n. 21.

[7] Perhaps one source for the poem's title can be found in Part 8 of *Demon* in the lines: "Neyasny trepet ozhidan'ya, Strakh neizvestnosti nemoy, Kak budto v pervoe svidan'e Spoznalis's gordoyu dushoy."

INTRODUCTION

Lines 177-79 develop this theme by being a series of type VI; as already noted, such lines tend to be negative in content. Here line 177 follows that pattern, and the fact that lines 178-79 have the same rhythm suggests a connection between "mathematical aridity" and the facial features of the poet's father. Finally, we have a profound rhythmic contrast expressed in lines 181-82. Line 181 is a perfectly rigid type I with all the word boundaries corresponding to the iambic feet and, if that were not enough, weighty punctuation marks isolating each word. A more rhythmically inflexible line of iambic tetrameter is hardly imaginable. This is followed by a type VI, which states that the questions of line 181 are "unanswerable"—this, in my view, being the poet's cry of personal and rhythmic frustration at the rigidity of line 181, which represents his father. Many like examples of rhythmic expressiveness can be found throughout the poem.

There is one other aspect of rhythm I would like to point out. Lines similar rhythmically in a passage tend to be linked in other ways as well, either by rhyme (lines 74 and 76), or by syntactic parallelism (51-52), or by internal sound correspondences as well as rhyme and/or syntactic parallelism (70-72). Examples of these interrelationships are legion and it is impossible to say which of the three factors, rhythm, sound, or syntax, is dominant, nor does it matter since they are all perfectly and ingeniously blended.

Rhyme

The poem is rhymed throughout in alternating masculine and feminine rhymes (*abab* . . .) with occasional rhymed couplets introduced for variety. The one lengthy exception to the alternating masculine-feminine pattern is the middle section of Part 2 (lines 491-540), which is all masculine.[8] A handful of minor exceptions aside, Bely's rhymes are not sonically experimental in comparison, say, to Mayakovsky; generally they are exact rhymes which fall well within Symbolist standards. However, the rhymes are inventive, often with great semantic distance between rhymed words, making them exciting and interesting; and there are practically no weak or grammatical rhymes. Moreover, there are a number of internal rhymes (notably lines 807-8). Rhymes often bridge white spaces between stanzas and also bridge Parts 1 and 2.[9]

---

[8] This fact was noted previously by Karlinsky, op. cit., p. 68.
[9] The positioning of the white spaces is an unstable factor and differs to some extent be-

INTRODUCTION

What makes Bely's rhyming particularly striking, however, are the extended relationships that he develops by means of his rhymes. By "extended relationships" I mean sonic links that connect more than a single pair of rhymed words. These relationships follow one or more patterns.

1. Related masculine-feminine rhymes:
    Lines 1-4: gnóm/tómy/priyóm/idiómy
2. Extended use of a single rhyme:
    Lines 178-85: raskósy/voprósy/voprósy/ósy
3. Distant echoes—several related rhyme pairs separated by some distance:
    Lines 226-29: metóy/(biryuzóvoy)/zolotóy/(belogolóvoy)
    Echo-lines 250-52: róy/igróy
    Echo-lines 262-64: volnóy/vesnóy
4. Repeats of rhymed words:
    Lines 251-53: bystrotechnost'/vechnost'
    Lines 456-57: Vechnost'/bystrotechnost'
5. Extended play on a rhyme vowel:
    Lines 191-204: vyyu/entropiyu/igry/vikhri/miry/utikhli/letit/
    prytche/vzletit/Nitche/Kyuri/strui

Only one example has been given for each type, but many are to be found.

Among the interesting semantic links created by rhymes, one in particular seems to be singled out for special emphasis. This is the repeated rhyme of *Solov'yov* with *zov* and *slov* (and implicitly with *bogoslov*) as in these lines: 329, 332; 368, 369, 372; 400, 402; 584, 586; 1291 (with internal rhyme), 1293. Obviously the connections between the philosopher and the "calls to eternity" and the "word" with its link to the Logos (see lines 386-89) form the thematic crux of the work and this is suitably expressed in the rhymes.

---

tween full editions of the poem. Furthermore, in the reprinting of sections of the poem in his collections of verse, Bely often arranged them in quatrains. It is therefore difficult to feel that the positioning of white spaces is an overly important factor in the poem.

Excerpts from *Pervoe svidanie* (with line numbers given in parentheses) are to be found reprinted with some changes in the following places: *Zapiski mechtateley*, 1922, no. 5, p. 46 (1028-43); A. Bely, *Stikhotvoreniya*, 1923, pp. 202-5 (773-805), pp. 305-6 (491-506), pp. 307-9 (509-40), pp. 311-12 (932-62), pp. 314-15 (99-146), pp. 318-20 (1134-93), pp. 321-22 (1028-55), pp. 440-42 (1238-61). In addition, the poem "Kladbishche" (A. Bely, *Zoloto v lazuri*, 1904, p. 174) found its way, in revised form, into lines 525-36 of *Pervoe svidanie*.

INTRODUCTION

Somewhat related to the matter of rhymes is the fact that, though the vocabulary of the poem is far-ranging, idiosyncratic, and from various stylistic levels, it is also, paradoxically, rather narrow and repetitive. Many words are repeated frequently in the course of the poem, often in rhyme position. Certainly, the third and fourth relationship patterns described above would not be possible without this. These much-used words are the thematic building blocks of the poem, which then is partly a product of play with these words in multifarious transformations and permutations.

Imagery

Under the rubric of imagery, I want to consider briefly Bely's uniquely profound penetration into the "hidden" essence of the word. The word for Bely was a powerful expressive entity, and he believed in confronting and making maximum artistic use of all attributes of the word—its sound, rhythm, even its visual aspect, and not just its denotation and connotation. This led to strikingly original thought patterns based as much on sound as on meaning. Associations resulting from rhymes are one type of such a pattern common in poetry, however Bely went much farther than most poets in his imaginative investigation of his verbal materials. A brief example is line 723: *Iz vóli: tólstye volý* . . . The association of *volya* (the will) with *vol* (ox) seems at first to be odd, without evident meaning. The most obvious reason for the connection is perhaps the similarity in sound. This is not, however, quite an internal rhyme because of the differing stress and the softness of one *l* and the hardness of the other. But the visual image of the two words is more similar than the sound. Semantically, the association is suggestive: the ox is a hardworking beast and it is a satisfying image of the will. Furthermore, the image occurs in a paradigm (lines 721-24) of similar associations: thought-eagle/heart-lion/will-ox/sound-world. In such a context, the picture can be broadened out to bring in the Evangelists, astrology, other associations with these animals, and also lines 18-21, where the same animals appear.

Another example is one founded on a series of rhymes: Lines 869-873 have the rhymes *valtorn/khorom/Norn/voron*. Unless the orchestra is actually playing something from Wagner's *Die Götterdämmerung*, in which the Norns appear in the opening scene of the prologue (what is being played is never specified), the association of horns and Norns is evidently

INTRODUCTION

due to the rhyme. Wotan's "raven" follows from the evocation of the Norns and brings us to the end of the opera where the ravens figure in Brünnhilde's immolation scene. However, the association of the sounds of horns and bassoons with the sounds of the Norns' speeches and the raven's cawing receives more profound support *within* the lines in question. We have links to "speech" based on semantics (razgovor [869]/rech' [871]), morphology (proritsayut [870]/rech' proro*cheskaya* [871], and sound (razgo*vor*/*vor*on [872]). In addition, a mood of seriousness and fatefulness echoes in all four lines. The Norns, of course, are prophesying doom, and Wotan's raven appears at the destruction of Valhalla.

A final example: Lines 975-978 develop the association of the rhymes *árfy*/*Márfy*. The connection between Martha and the harp is puzzling, but the thought process seems to be: harp-harpstring-heartstring (soul-string)-emotional reaction-Martha's emotional reaction to seeing Mary: the mundane world being witness to a manifestation of the divine (music, possibly also Zarina). In succeeding lines, *harp* is rhymed internally with *scarf* and the Marys and Marthas become part of the audience at the concert.

The foundation for Bely's thought processes is primarily verbal, not material, i.e. associations are based on internal properties of the words rather than on the external world, on the sign rather than on the referent. As a result, while his images are fresh and unique, and though they may be idiosyncratic, they are linguistically viable and imaginatively stimulating.

The sum of all the above-considered effects is a magnificent incantation. The memory of the past is, as Bely indicates in the Prologue, conjured from the depths by the majestic power of language. This power in the poet's hands is well-nigh inexhaustible.

Gerald J. Janeček
LEXINGTON, KENTUCKY

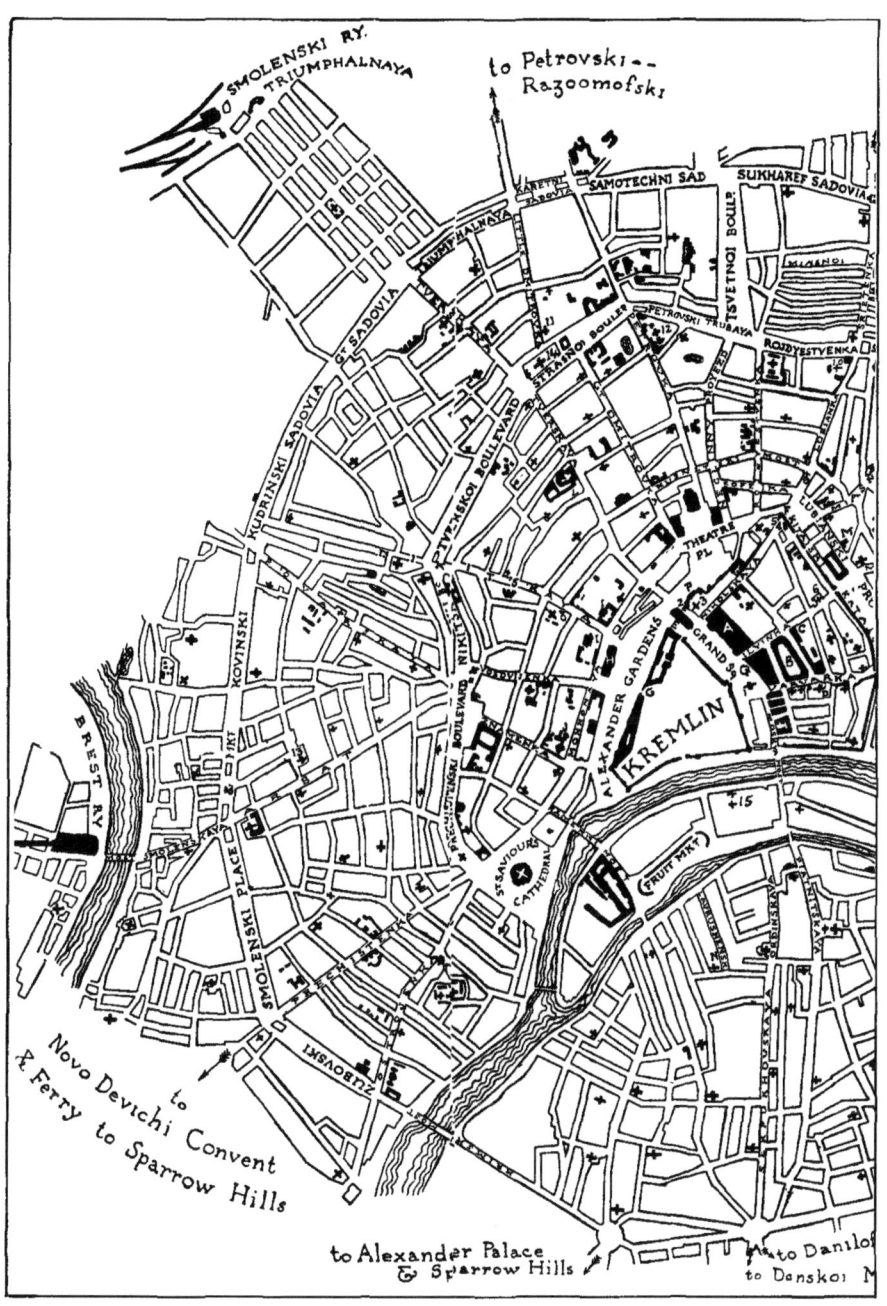

1. Map of Moscow, ca. 1912

PRELIMINARY REMARKS

*To the memory of Vladislav Khodasevich,
who left me the tuning fork.*

Andrey Bely's poem *The First Encounter (Pervoe svidanie)* is written in iambic tetrameter, the meter used overwhelmingly and successfully, by every Russian poet from Lomonosov through Pushkin, Tyutchev and Blok to Brodsky. The syllabo-tonic line based on the number of syllables and the number of stresses (or accents, beats, ictuses) produced stupendous results probably never expected from a binary meter. This fact has impeded and hampered the advent in Russia of blank verse and vers libre. (I am speaking here and elsewhere of blank verse not in the narrow English sense—unrhymed iambic pentameter—but in the broad sense of unrhymed verse of any meter, as it is understood in Russian and French prosody.) These forms remained underdeveloped. And although since Derzhavin's days (1743-1816) there has been a faint tradition of a more loose, less meter-oriented line (which in Russian is called *páuznik*), this "license" if used had to be motivated, at least in the first fifty years of its existence (see Derzhavin's "Ode to the Memory of General Bíbikov" and Semyón Bobróv's Preface to his *Khersonída* where the motivations are so touching and naive as to surpass anything written in the theory of verse). The tradition of vers libre and blank verse started its conscious development only during the great era of Symbolism (1890-1930), and Russian modernist poetry (1910-35).[1]

I do not intend to speak here about the intricacies of the Russian prosody, the possibilities of blank verse and vers libre, about what could have been done, what has not been done, and what should be done. I will not go into discussions about different approaches to the characteristics of binary and ternary meters and the idiosyncrasies of those who argued about them from 1910 to 1926. *Pervoe svidanie* is written in four-foot

---

[1] Tynyanov was over-optimistic when he wrote: "It is time to say that vers libre has become the quintessential verse of our time" ("Rhythm as the Constructive Element of the Line," in *The Problem of Poetic Language*, Leningrad, 1924).

iambic, and I will comment on this meter insofar as it pertains to the poem.

With all its built-in problems, the four-foot iambic served Russian poetry for two hundred years. From 1739 (Lomonosov's "Óda na vzyátie Khotiná") to 1930 or perhaps 1939, the iamb was the glory of Russia and the symbol of its vitality. As a sample of an early and brilliant discussion of Russian meter, I will only quote a short paragraph by Viktor Zhirmunsky, and then go on to Bely's poem. Zhirmunsky wrote:

> In poetry the rules of rhythm are realized in an uniform alternation of strong and weak syllables united in phonic series which repeat themselves. These rules of alternation are expressed by a definite metric scheme. The actual rhythm of the line deviates from the scheme—here as in all arts conformity never reaches the rigidity of a mathematical law. The basic plan that the metric scheme expresses, the basic movement, or the "impulse" (as O. Brik calls it) is felt in the verse as a whole, no matter how often we encounter the "deviations." First we see in the metrical pattern only the forming of the sound system, the "phonetic" structure which is felt by the rhythmic alternations of the strong and weak syllables. To this however are immediately added other elements in their structural order, elements of language-material. The basic metric impulse grasps all other elements of creative speech by its energy, and gives to the formless chaotic mass its structural unity and essential harmony.... (V. Zhirmunsky, *The Structure of Lyrical Poetry*, St. Petersburg, Opoyaz, 1921, p. 8.)

The Russian language requires that each word, no matter how short, have a stress, and only *one* stress—no matter how long the word. The short Russian words are like other short words in any Indo-European language, and there is not much that should be said about them (at this stage). But the long words are unusually long, and are not, as in English, stigmatized as "unnecessary" or "sophisticated," but are very much "in." They deserve to be given some attention here:

> *Vývernutye* (turned inside out)—stress on first syllable
> *Dovól'stvovat'sya* (to be satisfied)—stress on second
> *Sootéchestvennik* (countryman)—stress on third

PRELIMINARY REMARKS

Velikolépie (magnificence)—stress on fourth
Slovosochetánie (set expression)—stress on fifth
Kolenopreklonyónny (on one's knees)—stress on sixth

How does one use these words in a binary meter that is obviously intended to accommodate in its line (¯ ´ ¯ ´ ¯ ´ ¯ ´) four words of two syllables each?

The answer to this is at the core of Russian prosody. The ratio of words of three and more syllables to words of two syllables and less is three to two in the Russian language. Thus, the tremendous part that the *pyrrhic* (the unstressed binary foot, the "scud" in Nabokov's terminology), i.e. ¯ ¯, plays in Russian verse. This means that the iambic line (¯ ´ ¯ ´ ¯ ´ ¯ ´) with its hard ta-túm, reminding one of the marching drill of a military unit, becomes a fiction, and that Russian poems are infested with up-beats (unstressed syllables), which destroy the "regular" iambic line. This "destruction" becomes, indeed, the main rhythmic effect in Bely's poem where the pyrrhic plays the most prominent and striking role, although occasionally a spondee or a trochee comes along. Bely himself (in his *Ópyt análiza chetyryokhstópnogo yámba*) wrote extensively and in detail about the impact of the up-beats in Russian poetry. It is one of his major contributions to poetics, a landmark in Russian poetic theory, and was published in his collection of essays *Símvolizm* (1910).

What then would be a reasonable amount of these pyrrhics in a four-foot iambic line? There is no reasonable amount, answered Bely; the principle is: the more the better. The word-stress is the only thing that leads the poet through the tetrametric line, and this is paramount for the rhythm created by him in the frame of the meter. And therefore it becomes obvious that polysyllabic words give the Russian iambic verse not the figure

$$\bar{\ }\acute{\ } \quad \bar{\ }\acute{\ } \quad \bar{\ }\acute{\ } \quad \bar{\ }\acute{\ }$$

but more often than not

$$\bar{\ }\bar{\ } \quad \bar{\ }\acute{\ } \quad \bar{\ }\acute{\ } \quad \bar{\ }\acute{\ }$$

or $\quad \bar{\ }\acute{\ } \quad \bar{\ }\bar{\ } \quad \bar{\ }\acute{\ } \quad \bar{\ }\acute{\ }$

or $\quad \bar{\ }\bar{\ } \quad \bar{\ }\acute{\ } \quad \bar{\ }\bar{\ } \quad \bar{\ }\acute{\ }$

or $\quad \bar{\ }\bar{\ } \quad \bar{\ }\bar{\ } \quad \bar{\ }\acute{\ } \quad \bar{\ }\acute{\ }$

or $\quad \bar{\ }\acute{\ } \quad \bar{\ }\bar{\ } \quad \bar{\ }\bar{\ } \quad \bar{\ }\acute{\ }$

or $\quad \bar{\ }\acute{\ } \quad \bar{\ }\acute{\ } \quad \bar{\ }\bar{\ } \quad \bar{\ }\acute{\ }$

(and—as an ironic surprise—the line of Selvínsky: ¯ ¯ ¯ ¯ ¯ ¯ ¯ ´, and a joke in Bely's *The First Encounter*: ⁻ ´ ⁻ ⁻ ⁻ ´ ⁻ ⁻ in line 785). These are the many combinations of up-beats and down-beats in Russian tetrameter.

The results of such a discovery were brutal and came sooner than expected (and in an unanticipated way): Bely started to rewrite his early poems (1902-9) replacing two or three monosyllables with one polysyllable, thus glorifying the binary unstressed foot. Devoted friends begged him not to destroy what was already beautiful. But to no avail.

Although we still cannot accept his later versions, we certainly can sympathize with his anguish: the minor poets that came in the steps of Nekrásov (1821-77), and whom one is tempted to call poetasters, learned the rule of Písarev (the radical critic, 1840-68), whose conviction it was that the less poetry is poetry, and the more easy it can be scanned for practical purposes (marching along or sawing timber), the more useful it becomes for mankind. "Simple" prose should be the aim of all verse. The guru of the sixties and seventies ruined Russian poetry with his demand to write "with a social purpose," "to sing the misery of the people," "to wage war against the government," and get rid of all "superfluous embellishments." The poets of the seventies and eighties became the precursors of those who ninety years later were praised by Khrushchev because "their poems were fit to be sung by the Red Army Chorus."[2]

The word *monotony* was not used by Bely, but it was implied in his analysis of the Russian tetrameter in the period between 1850-90: the four-foot iambic had possibilities, and Bely saw them clearly and was eager to exploit them. Pushkin, Tyutchev, Fet (the last two extremely unpopular among their contemporaries) and the Symbolists, and others before and after them, tried to create—perhaps unconsciously, so he said—their own patterns of rhythm beyond the rigid rules of the meter. It is time, said Bely, to make *deliberate* changes in the rhythmic structure of the binary line.

The very beginning lines of *The First Encounter* have been given the following rhythmic pattern in its tetrametric straitjacket:

```
- /     - -     - /     - /
- /     - /     - /     - / -
/ -     - /     - -     - /
- -     - /     - -     - / -
```

---

[2] A mid-nineteenth-century translation of Shakespeare into Russian has a preface in which the translator tells the reader that he tried to eliminate all the unnecessary metaphors to make the tragedy less complicated.

where only one line (the second) is a "regular iambic" (25 percent, Bely would have said), and all the others are "deviations."[3]

Very soon a problem arose: what to do with the one- (or sometimes two-) syllable words such as particles, prepositions, negative particles, conjunctions, that did not need any emphasis or stress (except in some special cases)? Could they be read as pyrrhics, i.e. without undue stress to make the line sound even less monotonous? The Russian language is strongly inflected and the endings of declined nouns already give the ear the required meaning. Could such "trifles" as (giving here the English equivalents of Russian words) *on*, *of*, *and*, *in*, *by*, *re-*, *up-*, etc. be permitted to be "swallowed"? Did not the words that came immediately after indicate their own semantic stand by their grammatical endings?

Yes, they could, said Bely. Slur them in pronouncing them. Give them an up-beat. And what about the possessive pronouns? In Russian they are generally slurred anyway if there are no semantics involved: "I *took* (my) hat" but "I took *my* hat (not yours)." The possessive pronoun could become a pyrrhic, too, was the answer. (Nobody objected.) But then it dawned on him that even the personal pronoun was not *that* important: the Russian language has genders and numbers in verb conjugation, and the endings in the verb forms "I learn, we learn," or "he learns, she learns" are all different. They give the important information of masculine, feminine, singular, and plural. Why push the voice into a downbeat when a slur would be more appropriate, creating a beautiful pyrrhic?

line 234:   ⌣ ́ ⌣ ́ ⎼ ⎼ ́ ,   and not ⌣ ́ ⌣ ́ ⌣ ́ ⌣ ́
line 1232: ⎼ ⎼ ́ ⎼ ⎼ ́ ,   and not ⌣ ́ ⌣ ́ ⎼ ⎼ ́
line 1238: ⎼ ⌣ ́ ⌣ ́ ⎼ ́ ,   and not ⌣ ́ ⌣ ́ ⌣ ́ ⌣ ́

And this was how an ambitious "semi-scud" (Nabokov's later term) joined the crowd of the pyrrhics.

But how was all this poetry really read? How did the Symbolists and the great poets of the nineteenth century read their verse? What was the tradition, if there ever was one? What were the deviations allowed? What were the departures within the limits of law? What role was played by inversions for the sake of an additional up-beat; and how was the syntax strained to make a line sound more exquisite? I will try to answer these

---

[3] Here I follow Bely's terminology and not Zhirmunsky's who later came to the conclusion that the deviation *was* the pattern, the organic foundation of Russian iambic, inherent in the Russian language.

questions: I had the privilege of hearing every eminent Russian poet (between 1915 and 1930) read his poetry, everyone with two exceptions: Annensky, who died before my time, and Mandelstam, whom I never met. I heard Blok, Kuzmin, Sologub, Akhmatova in 1915 (I was 13), Bryusov in 1916, Gumilyov in 1921, Bely, Pasternak, Mayakovsky and Tsvetaeva in 1922-24, V. Ivanov in Rome in 1924, Balmont, Zinaida Gippius and Merezhkovsky in Paris in 1926, and of course Khodasevich. Tsvetaeva and the last four poets I heard until 1939.

Here I would like to mention the conversation that I had with D. S. Merezhkovsky in the thirties, which I recounted in my autobiography (*The Italics Are Mine*, New York, 1969, the Russian version, *Kursiv moy*). In his youth he had been well acquainted with two minor poets in their old age whom Turgenev had taught to recite Russian poetry "in the Pushkin tradition." This was a subdued, highly controlled and slightly sing-song manner, and Merezhkovsky tried to reproduce it for me. The "unnecessary" words were slurred. And the unobtrusive, unostentatious style of pronouncing the lines immediately reminded me of *our* (post-Bely) way of reading, that is the manner of the 1920-30 era: no stress was placed on semantics, and the rhyming was allowed to float by itself.

(When I now recall these precious moments with Merezhkovsky, I cannot but think of an analogous scene, which also took place on four time levels: Cyril Connolly, in his book *The Evening Colonnade*, tells how Hall Caine [1853-1931] told him about Wilkie Collins [1824-89] telling him, Caine, how Coleridge told him, Collins, about his narcotic experiences.)

So what, then, was the tradition, or was there more than one?

There were four traditions for reading poetry in Russian. The first was the nursery-rhyme tradition, a childish scanning in reciting not only children's verse, but any verse, that would sound like a ditty. The half-literate would read with gusto *ta-túm*, *da-dí*, *da-dá*, *ta-tám*, putting stresses on every iambic foot, including not only particles and prepositions, but also giving long words additional accents, and making every poem sound like *eena meena mina mo*. This tradition still exists. Every poem read that way produces a comic and offensive effect.

The second is the Stanislavsky Theater tradition. The poetry sounds like prose when pronounced as in a casual monologue about having petty money problems, or an occasional bellyache. Some gestures are added.

There is pathos in the voice, a sigh now and then arises if the subject matter is melancholy. It produces a destructive and offensive effect.

The third tradition is the declamatory one. A lament is murmured (or yelled in the manner of Madame Poshlyópkina in Act IV of Gogol's *Inspector General*). For a solemn statement, the thunderous voice of the Very Important Person from Gogol's "Overcoat" is used. Mayakovsky in 1915 when reading (declaiming) his poems to Maxim Gorky made such a show that the famous writer was frightened, and was preparing himself if not for witnessing hysterics at least for hearing sobs. From the third row in Madison Square Garden one could hear the sound of Mr. Evtushenko's breast-beating during his recital. This produces a bathetic and offensive effect.

The fourth tradition is what Polónsky (1819-98) and Pleshchéev (1825-93) heard from Turgenev about Pushkin's reading. This is unequivocally based not on the sentence, but on the line. The unit is the line, no matter what the punctuation says, and regardless of the enjambement, which would be only slightly hinted at by the voice. And this is where the false pyrrhics start to play their part.

These "omitted" or "slurred" words that gave the Russian tetrameter a license to live on borrowed time and kept the old prosody from dying, vastly enriched the sound texture of the iambic in the first quarter of our century. Gradually, stealthily, an evolution started where even some regular adjectives became neglected by restrained and rhythmic voices. (These adjectives in our contemporary usage are called *redundant*, and so should they be called here.) If there was a "*blue* sea" or a "*dark* night" in a not-too-felicitous line, one would not make it over-conspicuous, one would "swallow" it to give more sound-space to the next word. These are "modest adjectives" in the terminology of O. Brik—but there are never modest participles! If in line 8 it was said that there was a snowstorm raging, why put an accent in line 18 on the *white* blizzard in the street? Did we all cheat ourselves and our audiences? I do not think so, and what is art without lofty cheating, anyway? We tried to create more diversity, feeling unconsciously that the ⁻ ′ ⁻ ′ ⁻ ′ pattern was coming to an end. And Bely in *Pervoe svidanie* has amazingly few "regular" lines. As a matter of fact, in reading his verse he used his own vague idiosyncratic melody, as did Gumilyov, Kuzmin, Balmont, and apparently Mandelstam. This melody was used by them only in reading their own poems; other poets were read in another, smoother, more even way. Gippius, Blok, Sologub and Khodasevich did not use any melody. They read in a sober, gentle (and beautiful) tone and never made any distinction in reading their own or another poet's verse. Nevertheless, both groups (as with my own generation) belong to one "school" of reciting verse, whose initiator was heard by the young Turgenev, and the tradition of which is barely alive today.*

One basic law is clearly perceptible: no phrasal stress ever! Minimum punctuation transmitted by the voice! Use all the deviations that are "allowed," and also all those that are only "tolerated"! Some day a trend will start from this that Russian poetry needs badly: a new prosody where unrhymed lines will flow into the air "like down from the lips of Aeolus," and nonrestricted (free) verse will arise. They both are long overdue.

And now—the magnificent *First Encounter*, the work of a genius, the last in the line.

Nina Berberova
PRINCETON, NEW JERSEY

* These points are evident in a recently released recording from the Soviet Union that features Bely reciting his own verse, *Revived Voices* (restored recordings of 1908-1956), Melodıya 33M40—39857/58 (a).

АНДРЕЙ БЕЛЫЙ

ПЕРВОЕ СВИДАНИЕ

ПОЭМА

Алконост. Петербург. 1921.

2. Facsimile title page of the Alkonost edition, 1921

АНДРЕЙ БЕЛЫЙ

ПЕРВОЕ СВИДАНИЕ

ПОЭМА

1922

КНИГОИЗДАТЕЛЬСТВО «СЛОВО»

3. Facsimile title page of the Slovo edition, 1922

THE FIRST ENCOUNTER

ПРЕДИСЛОВИЕ.

    Киркою рудокопный гном
    Согласных хрусты рушит в томы...
    Я—стилистический прием,
    Языковые идиомы!
5   Я — хрустом тухнущая пещь,—
    Пеку прием: стихи—в начинку;
    Давно поломанная вещь,
    Давно пора меня в починку.
    Висок—винтящая мигрень...
10 Душа—кутящая...
                И—что же?...
    Я в веселящий Духов День
    Склонен перед Тобою, Боже!

    Язык, запрядай тайным сном!
    Как жизнь, восстань и радуй: в смерти!
15 Встань—в жерди: пучимым листом!
    Встань—тучей, горностаем: в тверди!
    Язык, запрядай вновь и вновь!
    Как бык, обрадуй зыком плоти:
    Как лев, текущий рыком в кровь,
20 О сердце, взмахами милоти!
    Орел: тобой пересекусь...
    Ты плоти—жест, ты знанью—числа...
    «Ха» с «И» в «Же»—«Жизнь»: Христос Иисус—
    Знак начертательного смысла...
25 Ты в слове Слова—богослов:
    О, *осиянная Осанна*
    Матфея, Марка, Иоанна—
    Язык!.. Запрядай: тайной слов!

    О, не понять вам, гномы, гномы:
30 В инструментаций гранный треск—
    Огонь, вам странно незнакомый,
    Святой огонь взвивает блеск.

PROLOGUE

    With pick in hand a miner-gnome
    Crumbles the consonant crackle into tomes . . .
    I'm—a device of style,
    The idioms of our language!
5 A hearth extinguishing in crackles—
    I bake devices: verse—for stuffing;
    A long-since broken apparatus,
    My overhaul is overdue.
    My temples are—a whirling migraine . . .
10 My soul—a-reveling . . .
                And yet,
    On merry Holy Spirit Day
    I am prostrate before you, Lord!

    My tongue, leap high by secret dreaming!
    Like life itself, arise, give joy: in death!
15 Rise—from a dead twig: as a swelling leaf!
    Rise—stormcloud, weasel: in the firmament!
    My tongue, leap high again, again!
    A bull, regale us with a carnal bellow:
    A lion, roaring in our blood,
20 O heart, with lambskin sweeps!
    Eagle: through you my days shall end . . .
    You are—to flesh the gesture—to knowledge the numbers .
    "X" and "I" into "X" is "Life": Christ Jesus—
    A sign of calligraphic meaning . . .
25 In the Word's word you are—a theologian:
    O, radiant Hosanna
    Of Matthew, Mark, and John—
    My tongue! . . Leap high: by word mystery!

    Gnomes, you will never understand:
30 Into a facet crash of instrumentation—
    The fire, strangely unfamiliar to you,
    The sacred fire shoots up sparkles.

1.

    Взойди, звезда воспоминанья;
    Года, пережитые вновь:
35 Поэма—первое свиданье,
    Поэма—первая любовь.
    Я вижу—дующие зовы.
    Я вижу—дующие тьмы:
    Войны поток краснобагровый,
40 В котором захлебнулись мы...
    Но, нет *вчера* и нет *сегодня*:
    Все прошлое озарено,
    Лишь песня, ласточка Господня,
    Горюче взвизгнула в окно...
45 Блести, звезда моя, из дали!
    В пути года, как версты, стали:
    По ним, как некий пилигримм,
    Бреду перед собой самим...
    Как зыби, зыблемые в ветры,
50 Промчите дни былой весны,—
    Свои ликующие метры,
    Свои целующие сны...

    Год—девятьсотый: зори, зори!..
    Вопросы, брошенные в зори...

55 Меня пленяет Гольбер Гент [1]...
    И я—не гимназист: студент...
    Сюртук—зеленый, с белым кантом;
    Перчатка белая в руке;
    Я—меланхолик, я—в тоске,
60 Но выгляжу немного франтом;
    Я, Майей мира полонен,
    В волнах летаю котильона,
    Вдыхая запах «poudre Simon»,
    Влюбляясь в розы Аткинсона [2].

---
[1] Английский прерафаэлит.
[2] «Уайт-роза»—духи фабрики Аткинсона.

1.

Ascend, O star of recollection;
The years experienced anew:
35 My poem is—my first encounter,
My poem is—first love.
I see—the gusting calls.
I see—the gusting darknesses:
The scarlet-red deluge of a war
40 In which we've choked ourselves . . .
But there is no *"today,"* no *"yesterday"*:
And all our past is illuminated,
Only the song, the good Lord's swallow
Screeched burning into my window . . .
45 Sparkle, my star, out of the distance!
The years, like milestones, mark our road:
Along it, like some unknown pilgrim,
I trudge before my very self . . .
Like ripples rippled in the winds,
50 Dash past, you days of spring gone by,—
Those triumphant rhythms of yours,
Those caressing dreams of yours . . .

The year is—nineteen hundred: dawns, dawns! .
Our questions flung into the dawns . . .

55 Holman Hunt[1] captivates me . . .
And I'm—no high-school student: a collegian . .
My frock coat—green, with piping—white;
A white glove in my hand;
I'm melancholic, I'm—in anguish,
60 But look a bit the dandy;
In thrall to Maya of the world,
I fly on a cotillion's waves,
Inhaling scents of "poudre Simon"
In love with rose perfume by Atkinson.[2]

[1] The English Pre-Raphaelite.
[2] "White Rose"—a perfume by the Atkinson Co.

65 Но, тексты чтя Упанишад,
Хочу восстать Анупадакой [3],
Глаза таращу на закат
И плачу над больной собакой;
Меня оденет ройАнанд [4]
70 Венцом таинственного дара:
Великий духом Даинанд [5],
Великий делом Дармотарра [6]...

Передо мною мир стоит
Мифологической проблемой:
75 Мне Менделеев говорит
Периодической системой;
Соединяет разум мой
Законы Бойля, Ван-дер-Вальса —
Со снами веющего вальса,
80 С богами зреющею тьмой:
Я вижу огненное море
Кипящих веществом существ;
Сижу в дыму лабораторий
Над разложением веществ;
85 Кристаллизуются растворы
Средь колб, горелок и реторт...
Готово: порошок растёрт...

Бывало,— затеваю споры...

Пред всеми развиваю я
90 Свои смесительные мысли;
И вот — над бездной бытия
Туманы темные повисли...

---

[3] «Анупадака»— безначальный: высокая ступень посвящения.
[4] «Ананда»- ученик Будды.
[5] Суами Сарасвати Даинанд — проповедник Индии XIX столетия
[6] Дармотарра— буддийский логик, последователь и комментатор философа Дармакирти (школа Дигнаги).

65   Revering the Upanishads,
       I want to resurrect as an Anupadaka,[3]
       I look agape upon the sunset
       And weep for an afflicted dog;
       A swarm of Anandas[4] will garb me
70   In garlands of a secret gift:
       Dhainand,[5] great in spirit,
       And Darmotarra,[6] great in deeds . . .

       Before me stands the world,
       A mythological dilemma:
75   For Mendeleev speaks to me
       Via his Periodic System;
       My mind amalgamates
       The laws of Boyle and van der Waals—
       With dreams of wafting waltzes,
80   And gods in ripening darkness:
       I see a fiery sea
       Of beings seething with quintessence;
       I sit in laboratory smoke
       Over the dissolution of a substance;
85   Solutions have been crystallizing
       Amid retorts, flasks, bunsen burners . . .
       That's it: the powder now is crushed . . .

       And I recall,—I'd start disputes . . .

       In front of everyone I explicate
90   Eclectic cogitations;
       And then—above the abyss of existence
       Appear some darkish hazes . . .

---

[3] "Anupadaka"—without beginning: a high degree of initiation.
[4] "Ananda"—a disciple of Buddha.
[5] Swami Sarasvati Dhainand—a preacher of 19th-century India.
[6] Darmotarra, Buddhist logician—follower and commentator on the philosopher Darmakirti (school of Dignagi).

    — «Откуда этот ералаш?»
    Рассердится товарищ наш,
95 Беспечный франт и вечный скептик:
    — «Скажи, а ты не эпилептик»?

    Меня бывало перебьет
    И миф о мире разовьет...

    Жил бородатый, грубоватый
100 Богов белоголовый рой:
    Клокочил бороды из ваты;
    И—обморочил нас игрой.
    В метафорические хмури
    Он бросил бедные мозги,
105 Лия лазуревые дури
    На наши мысленные зги;
    Аллегорическую копоть,
    Раздувши в купол голубой,
    Он дружно принимался хлопать
110 На нас, как пушками, судьбой;
    Бросался облачной тропою,
    От злобы лопаясь,—на нас,
    Пустоголовою толпою,
    Ругая нас... В вечерний час, —
115 Из тучи выставив трезубцы,
    Вниз, по закатным янтарям,
    Бывало, боги-женолюбцы,
    Сходили к нашим матерям...

    Теперь переменились роли;
120 И больше нет метаморфоз;
    И выростает жизнь из соли;
    И движим паром паровоз;
    И Гревса Зевс—не переладит;
    И физик—посреди небес;
125 И ненароком Брюсов адит;
    И гадость сделает Гадес;

    —"Where did you get this hodge-podge?"
    And this would pique our friend,
95 The carefree dandy and eternal skeptic:
    —"Say, aren't you an epileptic?"

    Then he would interrupt me
    To explicate the cosmic myth . . .

    There lived a bearded, crudish
100 And hoary swarm of gods:
    With beards of wadding tufted;
    They—deceived us with their games.
    Into a metaphoric gloom
    They threw our meager brains,
105 While pouring azure sillinesses
    Onto the little glimmers of our thought;
    Having inflated allegoric soot
    Into a sky-blue cupola,
    They undertook a joint barrage,
110 Bombarding us with fate like cannons;
    Bursting with irritation,
    Out of a cloud they rushed at us,
    In an empty-headed crowd
    Abusing us . . . In evening hours,—
115 With tridents thrust from blackened clouds,
    Downward, through sunset ambers,
    The women-loving deities
    Descended on our mothers . . .

    But now the roles have changed;
120 And there are no more metamorphoses;
    And life grows out of salt;
    And steamships are propelled by steam;
    And Zeus—will not improve on Grevs;
    And a physicist is in the sky;
125 And Bryusov hells it up by chance;
    And Hades'll play a hateful trick

И пролетарий — горний летчик;
И — просиявший золотарь;
И переводчик — переплётчик;
130 И в настоящем — та же старь!

Из зыбей зыблемой лазури,
Когда отвеяна лазурь, —
Сверкай в незыблемые хмури
О месяц, одуванчик бурь!
135 Там — обесславленные боги
Исчезли в явленную ширь:
Туда серебряные роги,
Туда, о месяц, протопырь!
Взирай оттуда, мертвый взорич,
140 Взирай, повешенный, и стынь, —
О, злая, бешеная горечь,
О, оскорбленная ледынь!
О, тень моя: о, тихий братец,
У ног ты — вот, как черный кот:
145 Обманешь взрывами невнятиц;
Восстанешь взрывами пустот.
Но верю: ныне очертили
Эмблемы вещей глубины —
Мифологические были,
150 Теологические сны,
Сплетаясь в вязи аллегорий:
Фантомный бес, атомный вес,
Горюче вспыхнувшие зори
И символов дремучий лес,
155 Неясных образов законы,
Огромных космосов волна...

Так шумом молодым, зеленым, —
Меня овеяла весна;

And a proletarian is an empyrean aviator;
And the sewer-cleaner shines like gold;
And translators are bookbinders;
130 And in the present—it's the same old bunk!

From ripples of the rippled azure,
After the azure has been winnowed out,—
Shine into the unrippled gloom,
O crescent-moon, you dandelion of the storms!
135 There—the dishonored gods
Have disappeared in manifest expanses:
In that direction, moon,
O thrust your silver horns!
Gaze on from there, dead son of gazes,
140 Gaze on, you hanged one, and be chilled,—
O angry, frenzied bitterness,
O injured frigid mass!
O shadow mine: O quiet brother,
Like a black cat: right at my feet
145 You will deceive in bursts of incoherencies;
You will arise in bursts of emptiness.
But I believe: today the emblems
Of prophetic depth have outlined—
Both mythological realities
150 And teleological dreams,
Combining in a weave of allegories:
A phantom demon, an atomic weight,
Burningly flashing dawns,
A dense forest of symbols,
155 The laws of unclear images,
The wave of boundless cosmoses . . .

Thus with its young, green noise,—
Spring wafted over me;

Так в голове моей фонтаном
160　Взыграл, заколобродил смысл;
　　　Так вьются бисерным туманом
　　　Над прудом крылья коромысл;
　　　Так мысли, легкие стрекозы,
　　　Летят над небом, стрекоча;
165　Так белоствольные березы
　　　Дрожат, невнятицей шепча;
　　　Так звуки слова «*дар Валдая*»
　　　Балды, над партою болтая, —
　　　Переболтают в «*дарвалдая*»...

170　Ах, много, много «*дарвалдаев*» —
　　　Невнятиц этих у меня.
　　　И мой отец, декан Летаев,
　　　Руками в воздух разведя:
　　　«Да, мой голубчик, — ухо вянет:
175　«Такую, право, порешь чушь!»
　　　И в глазках крошечных проглянет
　　　Математическая сушь.
　　　Широконосый и раскосый
　　　С жестковолосой бородой
180　Расставит в воздухе вопросы:
　　　Вопрос — один; вопрос — другой;
　　　Неразрешимые вопросы...
　　　Так над синеющим цветком,
　　　Танцуя в воздухе немом,
185　Жужжат оранжевые осы.

　　　И было: много, много дум;
　　　И метафизики, и шумов...

　　　И строгой физикой мой ум
　　　Переполнял: профессор Умов [7].

　[7] Профессор физики Московского Университета в 900-тых годах.

Thus meaning in my head
160 Had seethed and frolicked fountainlike;
Thus swirl the wings of the libellulae
In beaded mist above the pond;
Thus thoughts, light dragonflies,
Are flying in the sky and chirring.
165 Thus are the white-trunked birches
A-trembling, whispering their incoherence;
And so the sounds of *"dar Valdaya"*—
Are chattered into *"darvaldaya"*
By dunces prattling at their school desks . . .

170 Ah, many, many *"darvaldayas"*—
Much of such incoherence do I have.
My father, Dean Letaev, says,
Throwing his arms up in the air:
"Yes, my young fellow,—it makes me sick:
175 Really, the rot you're talking!"
And a mathematician's aridity
Would peep out of his tiny eyes.
His nose was broad, his eyes were slanted,
His beard hair very coarse;
180 He'd range some problems in the air:
First problem; second problem;
Unsolvable, these problems . . .
Like this above a sky-blue flower
Some yellow jackets stridulate,
185 And dance in quiet air.

And there were: many, many thoughts;
And metaphysics, and plain noises . . .

My mind was overfilled
With Umov's[7] stringent physics.

[7] Moscow University professor of physics in the first decade of the 20th century.

190 Над мглой космической он пел,
    Развив власы и выгнув выю,
    Что пародоксами Максвелл [8]
    Уничтожает энтропию,
    Что взрывы, полные игры,
195 Таят томсоновые вихри [9],
    И что огромные миры
    В атомных силах не утихли,
    Что мысль, как динамит, летит
    Смелей, прикидчивей и прытче,
200 Что опыт — новый...

                    — «Мир — взлетит!»
    Сказал, взрываясь, Фридрих Нитче...

    Мир — рвался в опытах Кюри
    Атомной, лопнувшею бомбой
    На электронные струи
205 Невоплощенной гекатомбой;
    Я — сын эфира, Человек, —
    Свиваю со стези надмирной
    Своей порфирою эфирной
    За миром мир, за веком век.

210 Из непотухнувшего гула,
    Взметая брызни, взвой огня,
    Волною музыки меня
    Стихия жизни оплеснула:
    Из летаргического сна
215 В разрыв трагической культуры,
    Где бездна гибельна (без дна!), —
    Я, ахнув, рухнул в сумрак хмурый, —

    [8] Известный физик.
    [9] Томсон — английский физик, автор теории вихревого строения вселенной.

190 He sang above the cosmic haze,
    His hair afloat and neck out-thrust,
    That Maxwell[8] by his paradoxes
    Is eliminating entropy,
    That Thomson's vortices[9]
195 Conceal explosions, full of play,
    And that gigantic worlds
    Have not subsided in atomic forces,
    That thought, like dynamite, takes flight
    More boldly, whimsically and nimbly,
200 That the experiment is—new . . .

                    —"The world—will burst!"
    Exploding, Friedrich Nietzsche said . . .

    The world's been bursting in Curie's experiments
    As an atomic bomb exploding
    Onto electron streams
205 Like an unconsummated hecatomb;
    I am—a son of ether, Man,—
    Down from the superterrestrial path
    I coil world after world, age after age
    With my ethereal royal purple.

210 Out of the unextinguished rumble,
    The material of life had splashed
    Against me, spraying me with fire
    And with a wave of music:
    Out of lethargic somnolence
215 Into the breach of our tragic culture,
    Where the abyss is fatal (bottomless!),—
    I gasped, collapsed into the gloomy dusk,—

    [8] Renowned physicist.
    [9] Thomson—English physicist, author of the theory of the vortical structure of the universe.

  — Как Далай-Лама молодой
  С белоголовых Гималаев, —

220 Передробряемой звездой,
  На зыби, зыблемые Майей...

  В душе, органом проиграв,
  Дни, как орнамент, полетели,
  Взвиваясь запахами трав,
225 Взвиваясь запахом мятели.
  И веял Май — взвивной метой;
  Июнь — серьгою бирюзовой;
  Сентябрь — листвою золотой;
  Декабрь — пургой белоголовой.
230 О, лазулитовая лень,
  О, меланитовые очи!
  Ты, колокольчик белый, — день!
  Ты, колокольчик синий, — ночи!

  Дышал граненый мой флакон;
235 Меня онежили *уайт-розы* [10],
  Зеленосладкие, как сон,
  Зеленогорькие, как слезы.
  В мои строфические дни
  И в симфонические игры,
240 Багрея, зрели из зари
  Дионисические тигры...
  Перчатка белая в руке;
  Сюртук — зеленый: с белым кантом...
  В меня лобзавшем ветерке
245 Я выглядел немного франтом,
  Умея дам интриговать
  Своим резвящимся рассудком
  И мысли легкие пускать,
  Как мотыльки по незабудкам;

[10] Духи.

   —As if I were the youthful Dalai Lama
   Out of the hoary Himalayas,—

220 Disintegrated by a star,
   On ripples, rippled by the Maya . . .

   As on an organ, playing though my soul,
   The days, an arabesque, flew on,
   Swirling in grassy fragrances,
225 Swirling in snowstorm fragrances.
   And May did waft—with upswirled fling;
   And June—with turquoise earring;
   September—with its golden leafage;
   December—with a hoary blizzard.
230 O lazulitian laziness,
   O those melanite eyes!
   You, little whitebell, are—the day!
   You, little bluebell, are—the nights!

   My cut-glass flacon breathed perfume;
235 *White Rose*[10] caressed me,
   Sweet green, like a dream,
   And bitter green, like tears.
   And in my strophic days,
   In my symphonic games,
240 Crimsoning, the Dionysian tigers
   Matured out of the dawn . . .
   A white glove in my hand;
   My frock coat—green: with piping—white . . .
   In wind which kissed me
245 I looked a bit the dandy,
   Who's skilled at fascinating ladies
   By his cavorting intellect,
   Releasing lightsome cogitations
   Like butterflies among forget-me-nots;

[10] The perfume.

250 Вопросов комариный рой
    Умел развеять в быстротечность,
    И—озадачить вдруг игрой,—
    Улыбкой, брошенною... в вечность...
    Духовный, негреховный свет,—
255   — Как нежный свет снегов нездешних,
        Как духовеющий завет,
        Как поцелуи зовов нежных,
        Как струн слова Заратустр,—

    Вставал из ночи темноколонной...
260 Я помню: переливы люстр;
    Я помню: зал белоколонный
    Звучит Бетховеном, волной;
    И *Благородное Собранье*,—[11]

    Как мир—родной (как мир весной),
265 Как старой драмы замиранье,
    Как то, что смеет жизнь пропеть,
    Как то, что веет в детской вере...

---

[11] Зал Благородного Собрания — Московский концертный зал в 900-тых годах.

250 I had the knack of wafting into fleetingness
    Mosquito swarms of questions,
    And—of confounding suddenly in play,—
    By smiles flung . . . into eternity . . .
    A spiritual and sinless light,—
255   —Like gentle light of other-worldly snows,
            Like an aroma-wafting testament,
            Like the caress of gentle calls,
            Like streams of the word Zaratustr,—

    Would rise out of dark-bosomed night . . .
260 And I recall: the chandelier cascadings;
    And I recall: the hall's white columns,
    The waves of Beethoven resounding
    In *Noblemen's Assembly Hall*,—[11]

    Like a familiar world (the world in spring),
265 And like the expiration of a dated drama,
    Like that which life dares sing *al fine*,
    Like that which wafts in childlike faith . . .

---

[11] The Noblemen's Assembly Hall—a Moscow concert hall in the first decade of the 20th century.

2.

На серой вычищенной двери
Литая, чищенная медь...

270 Бывало: пламенная вьюга;
И в ней—прослеженная стезь;
Томя предчувствиями юга,
Бывало, все взревает здесь;
В глазах полутеней и светов,
275 Мне лепестящих, нежных цветов
Яснеет снежистая смесь;
Следя перемокревшим снегом,
Озябший, заметённый весь,
Бывало, я звонился здесь
280 Отдаться пиршественным негам.
Михал Сергеич Соловьев,
Дверь отворивши мне без слов,
Худой и бледный, кроя пледом
Давно простуженную грудь,
285 Лучистым золотистым следом
Свечи указывал мне путь,
Качаясь мерною походкой,
Золотохохлой головой,
Золотохохлою бородкой,—
290 Прищурый, слабый, но живой.

Сутуловатый, малорослый
И бледноносый—подойдет,
И я почувствую, что—взрослый,
Что мне идет двадцатый год;
295 И вот, конфузясь и дичая,
За круглым ласковым столом
Хлебну крепчающего чая
С ароматическим душком;

2.

  Upon the gray and spotless door
  A polished cast-brass nameplate . . .

270 And I recall: a flaming blizzard;
  And there would be—a beaten path;
  With prescience of the human warmth,
  Here everything would come to life;
  A snowy mix of light and semishadows
275 Of petaled gentle flowers
  Lucidifies before my eyes;
  Leaving my tracks in drenching snow,
  All chilled and snow-encased,
  I ring the doorbell there
280 To give myself to sumptuous delights.
  Mikhal Sergeich Solovyov
  Opens the front door silently;
  Emaciated, pale, with blanket
  Clutched over his catarrhal chest,
285 By golden, luminescent
  Candle track, he shows the way;
  In rhythmic gait he rocks
  His golden-tufted head,
  His golden-tufted beard,—
290 Eyes squinting, weak, and yet alive.

  Stoop-shouldered, undersized
  And pale-nosed—he'd come up,
  And I would feel—adult,
  That I was in my twentieth year;
295 And then, becoming flustered and unsocial,
  While at the round and cosy table,
  I drink a cup of brisk
  And fragrant aromatic tea;

   Михал Сергеич повернется
300 Ко мне из кресла цвета «бискр»;
  Стекло пенснэйное проснется.
  Переплеснется блеском искр;
  Развеяв веером вопросы
  Он чубуком из янтаря,—
305 Дымит струями папиросы,
  Голубоглазит на меня;
  И ароматом странной веры
  Окурит каждый мой вопрос;
  И мне навеяв атмосферы,
310 В дымки просовывает нос,
  Переложив на ногу ногу,
  Перетрясая пепел свой...

  Он—длань, протянутая к Богу
  Сквозь нежный ветер пурговой!

315 Бывало, сбрасывает повязь
  С груди—переливной, родной:
  Глаза—готическая прорезь;
  Рассудок—розблеск искряной!
  Он видит в жизни пустоглазой
320 Рои лелеямых эмблем,
  Интересуясь новой фазой
  Космологических проблем,
  Переплетая теоремы
  С ангелологией Фомы;
325 И—да: его за эти темы
  Ужасно уважаем мы;
  Он книголюб: любитель фабул,
  Знаток, быть может, инкунабул,
  Слагатель не случайных слов,
330 Случайно не вещавших миру,
  Которым следовать готов
  Один Владимир Соловьев...

  Mikhal Sergeich turns to me
300 From his bisque-colored chair;
  His pince-nez glass has come alive,
  Awash with brilliant sparks;
  Arraying questions like a fan,
  Puffing his amber chibouk,—
305 He'd let out streams of smoke
  And flash his light-blue eyes at me;
  And with the incense of unique beliefs
  He'd fumigate my every question;
  And, having stirred the atmosphere,
310 He'd poke his nose into his smoke-puffs,
  Placing one leg upon the other,
  And flicking off his ashes . . .

  He is—a hand outstretched to God
  Through gentle blizzard winds!

315 And I recall, endearing, mutable,
  He'd throw the compress from his chest:
  His eyes—a Gothic latticework;
  His mind—a spark-dispersing splendor!
  He sees in our blank-eyed life
320 A swarm of cherished emblems;
  He's fascinated by new phases
  Of cosmological dilemmas,
  And interweaves his theorems
  With Thomas's angelology;
325 And—yes: for these same subjects
  We venerate him terribly;
  He is a bibliophile: a story-lover,
  A connoisseur of incunabula,
  Inventor of meaningful words,
330 Whose meaning was by chance lost on the world,
  And which Vladimir Solovyov alone
  Is ready to pursue . . .

                Я полюбил укромный кров —
                Гостеприимную квартиру...

335   Зимой, в пурговые раскаты
                Звучало здесь «На век одно»!
                Весною — красные закаты
                Пылали в красное окно,
                На кружевные занавески,
340   Лия литые янтари;
                Любил египетские фрески
                На выцветающих драпри,
                Седую мебель, тюли, даже
                Любил обои цвета «*бискр*», —
345   Рассказы смазанных пейзажей,
                Рассказы красочные искр.
                Казалось: милая квартира
                Таила летописи мира.

                О. М., жена его, — мой друг,
350   Художница —
                            — (в глухую осень
                Я с ней... Позвольте — да: лет восемь
                По вечерам делил досуг) —

                Молилась на Четьи-Минеи,
                Переводила де-Виньи;
355   Ее пленяли Пиринеи,
                Кармен, Барбье д'Оревильи,
                Цветы и тюлевые шали —
                Все переписывалась с «Алей»,
                Которой сын писал стихи,
360   Которого по воле рока
                Послал мне жизни бурелом;
                Так имя Александра Блока
                Произносилось за столом
                «*Сережей*», сыном их: он — мистик,
365   Голубоглазый гимназистик:

     I came to love this hidden shelter—
     This warm and friendly home . . .

335 In winter, into blizzard peals
     Resounded here "Forever one!"
     In spring—the reddish sunsets
     Were blazing through a reddened window,
     Onto the lacy curtains,
340 Showering smelted ambers;
     I loved the Egyptian frescoes
     On fading draperies,
     The hoary furniture, the tulles,
     I even loved the bisque wallpaper—
345 Tales told by modernistic landscapes,
     The multicolored tales of sparks.
     It seemed: the dear and kindly home
     Contained the chronicles of the world.

     O. M., his wife, is—my close friend,
350 A painter—
                —(during deepest autumn
     For . . . Let me think—that's right: eight years
     We spent our leisure evenings, she and I, together)—

     She reverenced the Cheti-Minei,
     And did translations of de Vigny;
355 She was enamored of the Pyrenees,
     Of Carmen and Barbey d'Aurevilly,
     Of flowers and tulle shawls—
     She corresponded constantly with "Alya,"
     Whose son wrote poetry,
360 Whom by the will of fate
     Life's tempest later sent to me;
     And thus the name of Alexander Blok
     Was uttered at the dinner table
     By their son, "*Seryozha*": a mystic,
365 A blue-eyed high-school boy:

О Логосе мы спорим с ним,
Не соглашаясь с Трубецким,
Но, соглашаясь с новым словом,
Провозглашенным Соловьевым
370 О «*Деве Радужных Ворот*», ¹)
О деве, что на нас сойдет,
Овеяв бирюзовым зовом,
Всегда таимая средь нас:
Взирала из любимых глаз.

375 «Сережа Соловьев»—ребенок,
Живой смышленый ангеленок,
Над детской комнаткой своей
Восставший рано из пеленок,—
Роднею Соловьевской всей
380 Он встречен был, как Моисей:
Две бабушки, четыре дяди,
И кажется, шестнадцать теть
Его выращивали пяди,
Но сохранил его Господь;
385 Трех лет, ну право же-с, ей Богу-с,—
Трех лет (скажу без лишних слов),
Трех лет ему открылся Логос,
Шести—Григорий Богослов,
Семи—словарь французских слов;
390 Перелагать свои святыни
Уже с четырнадцати лет
Умея в звучные латыни,
Он—вот, провидец и поэт,
Ключарь небес, матерый мистик,
395 Голубоглазый гимназистик,—
Взирает в очи Сони Н—ой,
Огромный заклокочив клочень;

¹ Гностический термин Софии, Премудрости, встречаемый в стихотворении Вл. Соловьева: «Не Изида Трехвенечная ту весну им принесет, а не тронутая, вечная, «*Дева Радужных Ворот*»...

      We have debates about the Logos, he and I,
      Not able to agree with Trubetskóy,
      But able to agree with new ideas
      Proclaimed by Solovyov
370 About the *"Maiden of the Rainbow Gate,"*[1]
      The maiden who will come upon us
      And waft a turquoise call;
      A mystery forever in our midst:
      She gazed from her beloved eyes.

375 "Seryozha Solovyov" is—a babe,
      A lively, clever little cherub;
      Early arisen from his diapers,
      Transcending his cute nursery,—
      By every member of his family
380 He was received like Moses:
      Two grandmothers, four uncles,
      And sixteen aunts, it seems,
      All cultivated his development;
      But God preserved him anyway;
385 At three, imagine, I swear it's true,—
      At three (I'll say it tersely),
      At three the Logos was revealed to him,
      At six—St. Gregory the Theologian,
      At seven years—a lexicon of French;
390 Aware from fourteen on of how
      To translate thoughts he held as sacred
      Into ringing Latin lines,
      Behold—a seer and a poet,
      Sacristan of the heavens, seasoned mystic,
395 A blue-eyed high-school boy,—
      He looks into the eyes of Sonya N—,
      From under his poofed pompadour;

[1] A gnostic term for Sophia, Wisdom, which is found in the poem by Vladimir Solovyev: "Not Isis, Thrice-Crowned, will bring them this spring, but the untouched, eternal *'Maiden of the Rainbow Gate'* " . . .

          Мне блещут очи—очень, очень—
          Надежды Львовны Зариной.
400   Так соглашаясь с Соловьевым,
          Провидим Тайную весной:
          Он—Сонечку, живую зовом;
          Я—Заревую: в Зариной...

          Она!... Мы в ней души не чаем...
405   Но кто она?... Сидим за чаем:
          Под хохот громкий пурговой
          Вопрос решаем роковой.
          Часы летят... Не замечаем...
          — «Скажи, тобой увлечена
410   «Надежда Львовна Зарина?...
          — «Не знаю я...»
                    — «Быть может?»
                              — «А?!»
          Михал Сергеич повернется
          Ко мне из кресла цвета «*бискр*»;
          Стекло пенснэйное проснется,
415   Переплеснется блеском искр;
          Его он сбрасывает кротко
          Золото-хохлой головой
          С золотохохлою бородкой
          Прищурый слабый, но живой;
420   И клонит кончик носа снова,
          В судьбу вопроса рокового:
          —«Надежда Львовна Зарина?
          «Как?!.. Воплощение Софии?...»

          — «В ней мне пророчески ясна
425   «Судьба священная России:
          «Она есть Львовна, дочка Льва;
          «Лев — символический, Иудин...

          — «Зарин, Лев Львович, — пошлый франт?
          «Безусый, лысый коммерсант?»

They sparkled at me—very much—
Nadezhda Lvovna Zarina's eyes.
400 Agreeing thus with Solovyov,
We foresee the Mysterious One in spring:
He—Sonechka, alive in her call;
I—my Irradiant One: in Zarina . . .

It's She! . . We are in love with her insanely . . .
405 But who is she? . . We sit at tea:
Outside the blizzard's raucous laughter
We work to solve the fateful problem.
The hours fly . . . We never notice . . .
—"So tell me, have you captivated
410 Nadezhda Lvovna Zarina? . ."
—"Don't know . . ."
    —"Might be, perhaps?"
        —"Oh, yes?!"
Mikhal Sergeich turns to me
From his bisque-colored chair;
His pince-nez glass has come alive,
415 Awash with brilliant sparks;
He throws it gently down,
Jerking his golden-tufted head,
His golden-tufted beard,—
Eyes squinting, weak, and yet alive;
420 And once again he pokes his nose
Into the fateful problem's destiny:
—"Nadezhda Lvovna Zarina?
What's that? ! . . The incarnation of Sophia? . ."

—"In her the sacred destiny of Russia
425 Is clear to me prophetically:
She's Lvovna, Leo's daughter:
The symbolic lion of the tribe of Judah . . ."

—"Zarin, Lev Lvovich, —the vulgar dandy?
A beardless, balding businessman?"

430 «Вопрос гностически не труден:
«Серапис, или Апис — бык,
«Таящий неба громкий зык,
«Есть только символ чрезвычайный
«Какой то сокровенной тайны...»

435 — «Ну хорошо, а что есть Лев?»

— «Иудин Лев — веков напев».
. . . .

Высокий, бледный и сутулый,
Ты где, Сережа, милый брат;
Глаза — пророческие гулы,
440 Глаза, вперенные в закат:
Выходишь в Вечность... на Арбат [2];
Бывало: бродишь ты без речи;
И мне ясней слышна, видна:
Арбата юная весна,
445 Твоя сутулая спина,
Твои приподнятые плечи,
Бульваров первая трава.
И вдруг: как на зеркальной зыбке
Пройдут пузыриками рыбки, —
450 Меж нами умные слова
И вовсе детские улыбки:
И разговор о сем, о том,
О бесконечности, о Браме,
О Вечности, огромной даме,
455 Перерастают толстый том;
И на Арбате мчатся в Вечность:
Пролеток черных быстротечность,
Рабочий, гимназист, кадет...;
Проходят, ветер взвив одежды,
460 Глупцы, ученые, невежды;

[2] Улица в Москве.

430 "The question is quite easy gnostically:
Serapis, alternately Apis, is—a bull
Concealing thundrous bellows of the sky,
He's just a symbol ultimately
Of some great hidden mystery . . ."

435 —"Well fine, and what's the lion then?"

—"The Judah lion is—the melody of ages."
. . . .

Stooped-over, tall and pale,
Seryozha, where are you, dear brother?
Your eyes—prophetic rumblings,
440 Eyes fixed steadfastly on the sunset:
You go into Eternity . . . on the Arbat;[2]
And I recall: you'd wander wordless;
And I could hear and see more clearly:
The youthful spring of the Arbat,
445 Your back stooped steeply over,
Your shoulders lifted upward,
The first green grass along the boulevards.
And suddenly: as if on rippling mirror-pond
Some minnows would swim by in bubbles,—
450 Between us sharp-witted exchanges
And wholly childlike smiles:
And conversation touching this and that,
About infinity and Brahma,
About Eternity, a monumental lady,
455 All this could fill a bulky tome;
On the Arbat there hurtles to Eternity:
A rapid stream of blackish carriages,
A worker, high-school boy, cadet . . . ;
They pass, the wind up-swirls their clothes,
460 Dolts, scholars, ignoramuses;

[2] A street in Moscow.

    Зарозовеет тихий свет
    С зеленой вывески: «*Надежды*» ³
    Над далью дней и далью лет...

    Смутяся уличною давкой,
465 Смутясь колониальной лавкой,
    Я упраздняю это все:
    «Мир — представление мое!»
    Ты — пламенный, в крылатке серой
    Средь зданий, каменных пустынь:
470 Глаза, открытые без меры, —
    В междупланетную ледынь,
    Свои расширенные сини
    Бросают, как немой вопрос,
    Под шапкой пепельных волос.

475 Бывало: за Девичьим Полем
    Проходит клиник белый рой;
    Мы тайну сладостную волим,
    Вздыхаем радостной игрой:
    В волнах лучистого эфира
480 Читаем летописи мира.
    Из перегаров красных трав
    В золотокарей пыли летней,
    Порывом пыли плащ взорван,
    Шуршат мистические сплетни...
485 Проходит за́-городом: лес
    Качнется в небе бирюзовом;
    Проснется зов: «Воамергес!»
    Пахнет: Иоанном Богословом...
    И — возникает в неба ширь
490 Новодевичий Монастырь.

    ³ Писчебумажный магазин на Арбате.

The quiet light starts being rosy
From the green signboard of: "*Nadezhda*"[3]
Above the vista of the days and years . . .

Confused by the street congestion,
465 Confused by the grocery store,
I do away with all of this:
"The world is—my Idea!"
You—flaming, in a long gray cape
Amid the buildings, the stone deserts:
470 Your eyes, immeasurably open,—
Fling into the interplanetary icy spaces,
Their blue, dilated irises
Like a mute question
From under locks of ashen hair.

475 And I recall: beyond Deviche Pole
A whitish swarm of clinics would go by;
We will the luscious mystery,
And sigh in joyful play:
In waves of radiant ether
480 We read the chronicles of the world.
Out of the red grass burning
Amid the golden-hazel dust of summer,
My coat exploding in a burst of dust,
The mystic gossip rustles . . .
485 We reach the city outskirts: woods
Would sway against a turquoise sky;
A call would rise: "Voanerges!"
A hint would come: of John the Divine . .
And—into the expanses of the sky
490 Novodevichy Convent would arise.

[3] A stationery store on the Arbat.

Огромный розовый собор
Подъемлет купол златозор;
А небо — камень амиант —
Бросает первый бриллиант;
495 Забирюзевший легкий пруд,
Переливаясь в изумруд,
Дробим зеркальною волной;
И — столб летает искряной...
Там небо бледное, упав,
500 Перетянулось в пояс трав;
Там бездна — вверх, и бездна — вниз:
Из бледных воздухов и риз;
Там в берега плеснет волной —
Молниеносною блесной...

505 Из мира, суетной тюрьмы, —
В ограду молча входим мы...

Крестов протянутая тень
В густую душную сирень,
Где ходит в зелени сырой
510 Монашек рясофорный рой,
Где облак розовый сквозит,
Где нежный воздух бирюзит;
Здесь сердце вещее, — измлей
В печаль белеющих лилей;
515 В лилово-розовый левкой
Усопших, Боже, упокой...

Присел захожий старичок,
Склонясь на палку... В ветерок —
Слетают скорбные листы;
520 Подъемлют сохлые кресты
Плач перебленных огоньков
И клянч фарфоровых венков.
Ты, сердце, — неумолчный стриж —
Кого зовешь, о чем визжишь?

The huge and pink cathedral
Would raise a cupola of gold-glints;
The sky—an amianthus stone—
Is casting its first diamond;
495 The slight pond turning turquoise,
Transfusing into emerald,
Is fractured by a mirror-surfaced wave;
And—then a sparky pillar flies . . .
The palid sky there, fallen,
500 Is girded in a belt of grass;
There are abysses now—above,—below:
Of palid chalice veils and chasubles;
It'd splash there like a wave at shore—
Just like a lightning-flashing spoon lure . . .

505 Out of the world, the jail of vanity,—
We pass in silence through the gate . . .

The shadows of the crosses are outstretched
Into the thick and sultry lilacs,
Where in the humid greenery
510 A swarm of nuns in habits walks,
Where clouds are rosily transparent,
Where gentle air turns turquoise;
Here, O prophetic heart,—abate
Into the sorrow of white lilies;
515 In lilac-rosy gillyflowers
To the departed grant eternal rest, Lord . . .

A little codger, dropping by, sat down
While leaning on his cane . . . And in the breeze—
The doleful leaves are falling downward;
520 The wizened crosses raise
Laments of faded little flames
And tinkling china garlands.
My heart,—incessant martlet—
Whom do you call, what do you screech about?

525 Кроваво-красная луна
Уже печальна и бледна...
Из церкви в зелени сырой
Проходит в кельи черный рой;
Рукопростертые кресты
530 Столпились в ночь... Приди же, Ты, —
Из прежних дней, из прежних лет!..
В часовне — цветоблеклый свет:
В часовне житель гробовой
К стеклу прижался головой;
535 И в стекла красные глядит,
И в стекла красные стучит.

Чуть фосфореющий из трав,
Сквозною головою встав, —
Подъемлет инок неживой
540 Над аналоем куколь свой...

. . . .
. . . .

О, незабвенные прогулки,
О, незабвенные мечты,
Москвы кривые переулки...
Промчалось все: где, юность, ты!..
545 Перемелькали наши взлеты
На крыльях дружбы и вражды
В неотрывные миголеты,
В неотразимые судьбы,
Чтоб из сумятицы несвязной,
550 И из невнятиц бытия
В тиски подагры неотвязной
Склонился лысиною я.
Зальются слабнущие светы
Под марамо́рохом [4] зимы

---

[4] Марамо́рохи — народное выражение: в значении «мороки».

525 The moon incarnadine is
    Already sad and pale . . .
    The black swarm passes on its way
    Through shrubs from church to cells;
    The arm-extended crosses
530 Have crowded into night . . . O come,—
    From prior days, from prior years! . .
    Within the chapel—a faded light:
    Within the chapel, a tomb inhabitant
    Presses his face to the red glass;
535 And through the glass he peers,
    And at the glass he taps.

    Nigh phosphorescent, having risen
    Out of the grass as a transparent head,—
    The dead monk elevates
540 His cuculla above the lectern . . .

    .   .   .   .
    .   .   .   .

    O unforgettable the strolls,
    O unforgettable the dreams,
    The crooked lanes of Moscow . . .
    It all has hurtled by: my youthful years! . .
545 Our flights have flitted past
    On wings of friendship and hostility
    Into uninterrupted flash-flights,
    Into our irresistible destinies,
    So that out of the disconnected babbling,
550 Out of the incoherencies of daily life
    Into the throbs of unremitting gout,
    I could sink my balding head.
    The failing lights would start a flow
    Beneath the winter mumble-jumble[4]

[4] "Maramorokhi"—a folk expression meaning "moroki."

555 Переливной струею Леты,
Незаливной струею тьмы...
Рассудку, рухнувшему, больно, —
Рассудку, тухнущему в ночь...
И возникают сны невольно,
560 Которых мне не превозмочь...

. . . .

Да, — и опора в детской вере,
И Провидения рука—
На этой вычищенной двери
Литая, медная доска:
565 *Михал Сергеич Соловьев*
(С таких то до таких часов).

. . . .

Здесь возникал салон московский,
Где из далекой мне земли, —
Ключевский, Брюсов, Мережковский
570 Впервые предо мной прошли.
Бывало: —
— снеговая стая —
Сплошное белое пятно —
Бросает крик, слетая, тая —
В запорошенное окно;
575 Поет под небо белый гейзер:
Так заливается свирель;
Так на эстраде Гольденвейзер [5]
Берет уверенную трель.
Бывало: в вой седоволосый
580 Пройдет из Вечности самой
Снегами строющий вопросы
Черноволосою космой, —
Захохотавший в вой софистик,
Восставший шубой в вечный зов, —
585 Пройдет «*Володя*», вечный мистик,

[5] Известный московский пьянист.

555 Just like the overflowing stream of Lethe,
   Just like the unfloodable stream of darkness .
   My mind, collapsed, is suffering,—
   My mind extinguishes into the night . . .
   And dreams arise unwittingly,
560 Which I cannot subdue . . .

   . . . .
   Yes,—support in childlike faith,
   And Providence's hand—
   Upon this very spotless door
   A polished cast-brass nameplate:
565 *Mikhal Sergeich Solovyov*
   (*From such-and-such to such-and-such o'clock*).

   . . . .

   And here arose the Moscow salon
   Where—from, to me, a distant land,—
   Klyuchevsky, Bryusov, Merezhkovsky
570 First came before my eyes.
   And I recall:—
                              —a snowy flock—
   Forming a dense white blotch—
   Would give a shout, descending, melting—
   At the beflurried window;
575 A white geyser sings right up to the sky:
   That's how the reed-pipe spouts its tune;
   That's how in concert Goldenweiser[5]
   Attacks a self-assured trill.
   And I recall: amidst the hoary howl,
580 There'd come out of Eternity itself
   Laughing into the howl of sophistries,
   With shaggy black-haired mane,
   Constructing questions out of snow,—
   Arising, dressed in fur, to the eternal call,—
585 "*Volodya*," the eternal mystic would pass by,

   [5] The renowned Moscow pianist.

Или — Владимир Соловьев...
Я не люблю характеристик,
Но всетаки... —
                        — Сквозной фантом,
Как бы согнувшийся с ходулей,
590 Войдет, и — вспыхнувшим зрачком
В сердца ударится, как пулей;
Трясем рукопожатьем мы
Его беспомощные кисти,
Как ветром неживой зимы
595 Когда то свеянные листья;
Над чернокосмой бородой,
Клокоча виснущие космы
И желчно дующей губой
Раздувши к чаю макрокосмы,
600 С подпотолочной вышины
Сквозь марамо́рохи и сны
Он рухнет в эмпирию кресла, —
Над чайной чашкою склонен,
Сердит, убит и возмущен
605 Тем, что природа не воскресла,
Что сеют те же господа
Атомистические бредни,
Что декаденты — да, да, да! —
Свершают черные обедни
610 (Они — пустое решето:
Козлят не с Музой — с сатирессой,
И увенчает их за то
Патриотическая пресса),
Что над Россией — тайный враг
615 (Чума, монголы, эфиопы),
Что земли портящий овраг
Грызет юго-восток Европы;
Стащивши пару крендельков
С вопросом: «Ну и что ж в итоге?»
620 Свои переплетает ноги
Грохочет парой каблуков.

In other words:—Vladimir Solovyov . . .
I don't like characterizations,
But anyway . . .—
                    —A transparent phantom,
As if he's bending down from stilts,
590 He would come in, and—with a flashing eye
Would hit men's hearts, as with a bullet;
In giving him a handshake, up and down
We jerk his helpless wrists,
Which are like leaves once blown down
595 By winds of lifeless winter;
Above his black, disheveled beard
He tousles his long hair;
A lip is biliously puffed out,
Blows macrocosmoses upon the tea;
600 Down from his ceiling height
Through all the mumble-jumble and the dreams
He would collapse into the empirics of an armchair,—
Bent down above his cup of tea,
Outraged, crushed, angry
605 That nature was not resurrected,
That those same gentlemen are sowing yet
Their atomistic nonsense,
That decadents—O yes, they are!—
Are consummating black masses
610 (They are—like empty sieves:
They satyrize with satyresses, not the Muse,
And they are crowned for doing this
With laurels from the patriotic press),
That there's a secret enemy attacking Russia
615 (A plague, the Mongols, Ethiopians),
And that a rank ravine of earth
Is gnawing at the southeast part of Europe.
While snatching several crullers
And querying: "So what will be the end result?"
620 He intertwines his legs—
And clatters with his pair of heels.

Судьба трагическая дышет
Атмосферическим дымком,
И в «Новом Времени» о том
625 Демчинский знает, но не пишет:
— «В сознаньи нашем кавардак:»
«Атмосферических явлений»
«Свечений зорь нельзя никак,
«Понять с научной точки зрений».
630 Он—угрожает нам бедой,
Подбросит огненные очи;
И—запророчит к полуночи,
Тряхнув священной бородой!..

Так в ночи вспыхивает магний;
635 Бьет электрический магнит;
И над поклонниками Агни,
Взлетев, из джунглей заогнит;
Так погромыхивает в туче
Толпа прохожих громарей;
640 Так плещут в зыбине летучей,
Сребрея, сети рыбарей.

За ним вдогонку—следом следом,
Михал Сергеич делит путь,
Безмолвный, ровный, кроя пледом
645 Давно простуженную грудь,
Потея в вязаной рубашке,
Со столика приняв поднос,
На столике расставив шашки,
Над столиком поставив нос;
650 И скажет в пепел папирос
В ответ на новости такие:
— «Под дымкой—все; и всюду—тень»...
«Но не скудеет Мирликия [6]...
«Однако ж... будет: Духов день!»

[6] Родина Николая Чудотворца: аллегорически — «Страна Чудес».

A tragic destiny is breathing
Our atmospheric haze,
About which in "New Times"
625 Demchinsky knows but doesn't write:
—"There's bedlam in our consciousness:
All atmospherical phenomena—
The aureolae of the sun
Can't be accounted for by science."
630 He—threatens us with a disaster,
And casts his fiery eyes around;
And—starts to prophesy toward midnight,
Shaking his sacred beard!..

Magnesium thus flashes in the night;
635 Or an electromagnet pulsates;
And flaring over Agni's worshipers,
The flames rush forth out of the jungles;
A crowd of passing thunder-men
Thus rumbles in a blackish cloud;
640 Thus splash the nets of fishermen,
While silvering in flying ripples.

Pursuing him—right on the track,
Mikhal Sergeich shares his journey,
Laconic, even-tempered, and with blanket
645 Clutched over his catarrhal chest,
Perspiring in his knitted shirt;
Having removed the side-table tray,
Having positioned checkers on a board,
He sets his nose above them;
650 And he would say into the ashes of his cigarette
In answer to such news:
—"Everything is—haze and shadows . . .
But Myrlykia[6] is still fertile . . .
In spite of all there'll be a Holy Spirit Day!"

[6] The homeland of St. Nicholas, the Miracleworker: allegorically—"The Land of Miracles."

655 Свой мякиш разжевавши хлеба,
Сережа Соловьев под небо
Воскликнет—твердый, как кремень:
— «Не оскудела Мирликия!..
«А ну-ка все, кому не лень,
660 «В ответ на дерзости такие,—
«В Москве устроим Духов день!»

Но Соловьев не отвечая,
Снедаем мировой борьбой,
Проглотит молча чашку чая,
665 Рукой бросаясь, как на бой,
На доску: он уткнется в шашки;
И поражают худобой
Его обтянутые ляжки;
Бывало он пройдет к шинели:
670 В меха шинели кроет взор;
И—удаляется в метели:
Седою головой в бобер;
А вихри свистами софистик
Всклокочут бледный кругозор!
675 Привзвизгнут: «Вот великий мистик!»
И—пересвищут за забор!

А мы молчим, одним объяты;
В веках—одно: навек одно...
А перезвоны, перекаты
680 Снежат, как призраки, в окно;
А лампа бросит в занавески,
Свои литые янтари;
Молчат египетские фрески
На выцветающих драпри.
685 Михал Сергеич повернется
Ко мне из кресла цвета «бискр»;
Стекло пенснэйное проснется
Переплеснется блеском искр...

655 Chewing his crustless bread,
Seryozha Solovyov, as hard as flint,
Would shout up to the sky:
—"Yes, Myrlykia is still fertile!..
Come on all you who're not too lazy,
660 In answer to such impudence
We'll organize a Holy Spirit Day in Moscow!"

But Solovyov, not answering,
Consumed with worldwide struggle,
Would down a cup of tea in silence,
665 Throwing his hand, as if to battle,
Toward the board: he'd lose himself in checkers;
He shocks us with the thinness
Of his attired thighs;
He'd go to get his overcoat:
670 And hide his eyes in his fur collar;
And—wander off into the blizzard:
Into the beaver collar with his hoary head;
But vortices like hisses of sophistries
Disturb the pale horizon!
675 They'd screech: "Here comes the mighty mystic!"
And—hiss away across the fence!

And we are silent, filled with one idea;
Throughout the ages—one: forever one . . .
The chimes, the snowy caterwauls
680 Fling snow, like ghosts, into the window;
The lamp casts smelted ambers
Against the window curtains;
And those Egyptian frescoes
Are silent on the fading draperies.
685 Mikhal Sergeich turns to me
From his bisque-colored chair;
His pince-nez glass has come alive,
Awash with brilliant sparks . . .

Он—канул в Вечность: без возврата;
690 Прошел в восторг нездешних мест:
В монастыре, в волнах заката,—
Рукопростертый, белый крест
Стоит, как память дорогая;
Бывало он,—оснёжен весь,
695 Светлеет, огоньком мигая;
Бывало, все взреевает здесь:
Играет скатерть парчевая,
Снегами воздухи взвивая;
И в ней—прослёженная стезь;
700 Хрустя перемокревшим снегом,
Бегу сюда отдаться негам,
Озябший, заметенный весь.

Так всякий: поживет, и—помер,
И—принят под такой-то номер.

He—sank into Eternity: without return;
690 He passed into the ecstasy of otherwordly places:
In waves of sunsets, in a convent,—
A white and arm-extended cross
Is standing like a precious memory;
And I recall, it,—all snow-covered,
695 Would shine, while flickering its flame;
Here everything would come to life:
The brocade of the lectern cover moves,
The blizzard wind disturbs the chalice veils;
And there would be—a beaten path;
700 Crunching my tracks in drenching snow,
I run to give myself to these delights,
All chilled and snow-encased.

Like everyone: he lived, and—died,
And—was assigned a number.

3.

705 Под стук сердец — «в концерт, в концерт» —
Мудрец, юнец. Но что их манит,
То — запечатанный конверт:
Словами тайными обманет;
Немой, загаданный глагол,
710 Неизрекаемый, — он волит:
То марамо́рохами зол,
То добрым делом соглаголет;
Изранит стуками минут,
Багрянит, звуками измуча, —
715 Такой мяукающий зуд,
Такая дующая туча!...

Звук множит бестолочь голов
И гложет огненное сердце;
И в звуках нет толковых слов;
720 Здесь не найдешь единоверца;
Из мысли: вылетят орлы;
Из сердца: выйдет образ львиный;
Из воли: толстые волы...
Из звука: мир многоединый.
725 Тот, звуковой, — во все излит;
Та, звуковая, — золотая;
И этот — камень лазулит;
И этот — пламенная стая.

  У той: —

  — Над златокарей згой
730 Град Гелиополь: дева Отис,
 Милуясь лепетной серьгой
 Целует цветик, миозо́тис;
 Рогами гранными, как чорт,
 Туда — в века, в лазури-ляпис —
735 Граниторозовый простерт
 В нее влюбленный, странный Апис.

3.

705 To heart's throbbings—"to the concert, to the concert"—
A sage, a youth. But what attracts them
Is—the program undisclosed:
It will deceive with its mysterious words;
A verbum mute and preordained,
710 Unutterable,—it wills:
Now it will speak with mumble-jumbles,
Of evils, now with a good deed;
It'll wound by throbs of minutes,
It'll redden, torturing with sounds,—
715 Such a meowing itch,
A gusting stormy cloud! . . .

Sound multiplies the muddle of heads
And gnaws the fiery heart;
In sounds there are no sensible words;
720 You won't find there a cobeliever;
Out of a thought: fly eagles;
Out of the heart: a lion's image will emerge;
Out of the will: fat oxen . . .
And out of sound: the many-in-one world.
725 This one, he's sound-filled, poured in everything;
And this one, she is sound-filled, golden;
And that one is a stone of lazulite;
And that one is a flaming flock.

Here is a woman:—

    —Above a gold-brown glimmer
730   The city Heliopolis: the maiden Otis,
    Caressed by murmuring earrings,
    Kisses a flower, miozotis;
    Enamored of her, puzzling Apis,
    Granite-pink, stretches his horns
735   Faceted, like the devil,
    Into the ages, into the lapis lazuli.

У этой: —

— вытечет титан,
Златоголовый, змееногий;
Отзолотит в сырой туман:
740 И — выгорит, немой и строгий;
Седое облако висит
И, молний полное, блистает,
Очами молний говорит,
Багровой зубриной слетает,
745 Громово тарарахнув в дуб
Под хохотом Загрея-Зевса...

Вот этот вот: он — туп, как... пуп:
Прочел — приват-доцента Гревса...

И дирижирует: Главач [1].
750 И дирижирует: Сафонов [2])...
И, фанфаронит: часто — врач;
И, солдафонит: каста «*фонов*»;
Интерферируя наш взгляд
И озонируя дыханье,
755 Мне музыкальный звукоряд
Отображает мирозданье —
От безобразий городских
До тайн безобразий Эреба,
До света образов людских
760 Многообразиями неба;
Восстонет в ночь эфирный пад,
В эонах гонит бури знаков:
Златокосых Ореад,
Златоколесых зодиаков...

. . . .

[1] Петербургский дирижер 900-х годов.
[2] Директор московской консерватории этого времени.

Here is another: for her—

        —a titan will flow out,
        Gold-headed, serpent-legged;
        He'll flash his gold into the mist:
740   And—then burn out, mute and stern;
        A hoary cloud is hanging there
        And, full of lightning, it is gleaming.
        It speaks with lightning-flashing eyes,
        Descends in crimson zigzags,
745   And crashes thundrously into an oak
        To the guffaws of Zeus-Zagreus . . .

And this man here: he's stupid as . . . a nincompoop:
He's read—the works of docent Grevs . . .

And the conductor is: Hlaváč.[1]
750 And the conductor is: Safonov . . .[2]
And here the M.D.s come: to show off;
A caste of Baltic barons: goes a-bullying;
While interfering with our view
And ozonizing our breathing,
755 The musical scale informs
For me the universe—
From urban deformation
To formless mysteries of Erebus,
And to the light of human forms
760 In multiformities of sky;
The falling stars will rise at night,
Will chase in eons storms of sighs:
Of golden-braided Oreads,
Of gold-wheeled Zodiacs . . .

. . . .

[1] A Petersburg conductor of the first decade of the 20th c.
[2] Director of the Moscow Conservatory at this time.

765 Стой — ты, как конь, заржавший стих —
Как конь, задравший хвост строками —
Будь прост, четырехстопен, тих:
Не топай в уши мне веками;
Ведь я не проживу ста лет...
770 Я — вот... Я — здесь: студент московский
Я — на подъезде...

      Люстры свет.
И — Алексей Сергеич П-овский...
И — сердца бег, и — сердца стук.
Сердца — бегут: на звуки... Верьте, —
775 В субботу вечером наш круг
На Симфоническом концерте...

Проходят, тащатся, текут;
Вокруг — шпалеры кавалеров:
Купцов, ученых, мильонеров
780 (Седых, муругих, пегих, серых!);
Марковников профессор — тут;
Бурбон... И — рой матрон «мегéрых»,
И — шу-шу-шу, и — ша-ша-ша,
И — хвост оторван: антраша...
785 Багровая профессорша;
За ней в очках профессор тощий
Несет изглоданные мощи
И — злое, женино боа;
Вот туалет Минангуá ³ :
790 Одни сплошные валансьены;
И — тонкий торс; и юбка «клошь», —
Не шумно зыблемая рожь,
Не шумно зыблемые пены;
Блистая ручкой костяной,
795 Взлетает веер кружевной...
О, эти розовые феи!..
О, эти, голубые!.. Ишь: —

---

³ Модная московская портниха 90-х годов.

765 Halt—you, a horse, my neighing verse—
A horse that swished his tail in lines—
Be artless, tetrametric, quiet:
Don't stomp the ages in my ears;
I will not live a hundred years, you know . . .
770 Look . . . Here—I am: a Moscow student,
At the main entrance . . .

                          The light of chandeliers.
And—Aleksey Sergeich P-ovsky . . .
My heart's flight, and—my heart's throb.
Hearts—fly: toward the sounds . . . Believe me,—
775 On Saturday nights our group
Is always at the Symphony . . .

They pass by, drag their feet, flow on;
Around—are squads of young gallants:
Of merchants, scholars, millionaires
780 (Whites, chestnuts, piebalds, greys!);
Markovnikov, Professor, he is—there;
A boor . . . And—swarms of haggish matrons,
And—hush, hush, hush, and—chatter, chatter, chatter,—
A train is torn off: entrechats . . .
785 Here is a crimson-faced professor's wife;
Behind, a gaunt, bespectacled professor
Is carrying his gnawed-out relics
And—his wife's vicious boa;
And there's a genuine Minangois[3] gown:
790 A solid mass of Valenciennes;
And—narrow waist; and skirt "cloche,"—
A field of lightly rippling rye,
A sea of lightly rippling foam;
A lacy fan flies up,
795 With ivory handle sparkling . . .
Oh, oh, these rosy fairies! . .
Oh, oh, these powder-blue ones! . . Look:—

[3] A fashionable Moscow dressmaker of the 1890s.

        Красножилетые лакеи
        Играют веером афиш.

800   Графиня толстая, Толста́я,
        Уж загляделась в свой лорнет...
        Выходит музыкантов стая;
        В ней кто то, лысиной блистая,
        Чихает, фраком отлетая,
805   И продувает свой кларнет...
        Возня, переговоры... Скрежет:
        И трудный гуд, и нудный зуд —
        Так ноет зуб, так нудит блуд...
        Кто это там пилит и режет?
810   Натянуто пустое дно, —
        Долдонит бебень барабана,
        Как пузо выпуклого жбана:
        И тупо, тупо бьет оно...

        О, невозможные моменты:
815   Струня́т и строют инструменты...

        Вдруг!...
                Весь — мурашки и мороз!
        Между ресницами — стрекозы!
        В озонных жилах — пламя роз!
        В носу — весенние мимозы!

820   Она пройдет — озарена:
        Огней зарней, неопалимей...
        Надежда Львовна Зарина
        Ее не имя, а — «*во-имя*»!..
        Браслеты — трепетный восторг —
825   Бросают лепетные слезы;
        Во взорах — горний Сведенборг;
        Колье — алмазые морозы;
        Серьга — забрежжившая жизнь;
        Вуаль провеявшая — трепет;

Red-jacketted attendants
Are flicking fans of programs.

800 The portly Countess Tolstoy
Is lost in looking through her lorgnette . . .
And the musician flock is entering;
Within it one, with baldspot sparkling,
Sneezes, his frock coat flapping outward,
805 And blows his clarinet to clear it . . .
Much bustle, words exchanged . . . And gnashing:
A snaggy rasp, and vexing itch—
Thus aches a cusp, thus sex insists . . .
Who is it sawing there and slicing?
810 The empty bottom is made taut,—
The drum da-duns, ba-booms,
As on the belly of a wooden jug:
And dully, stupidly it beats . . .

O, those insufferable moments:
815 They string and tune their instruments . . .

Suddenly! . .
                All—shivers, chills!
Between eyelashes—dragonflies!
In ozoned veins—a flame of roses!
And in my nostrils—spring mimosas!

820 She'd pass by—illuminated:
More fiery, unburnable than sunrise . . .
Nadezhda Lvovna Zarina
Hers not a name, but *"in-the-name-of"*! . .
Her bracelets—quivering ecstasy—
825 Throw off their murmuring tears;
And in her gazes—lofty Swedenborg;
Her necklace—diamantine frosts;
Her earrings—dawns of brilliant life;
Her fluttering veil—a shudder;

830 Кисей вуалевая брызнь
И юбка палевая — лепет;
А тайный розовый огонь,
Перебегая по ланитам
В ресниц прищуренную сонь,
835 Их опаливший меланитом, —
Блеснет, как северная даль,
В сквозные, веерные речи...
Летит вуалевая шаль
На бледнопалевые плечи.

840 И я, как гиблый Гибеллин,
У Гвельфов ног, — без слов, без цели:
Ее потешный палладин...
Она — Мадонна Рафаэля!
Пройдет, — мы, вспыхнувши, вздохнем,
845 Идиотически ослабнем...
Пройдет с раскосым стариком,
С курносым, с безволосым бабнем —
Пройдет, и сядет в первый ряд,
Смеясь без мысли и без речи [4];
850 И на фарфоровые плечи,
Переливаясь, бросят взгляд —
Все электрические свечи.
И ей бросает оклик свой —
Такой простой, — Танеев-мейстер [5];
855 Биноклит в ложе боковой
Красавец обер-полицмейстер [6].

Взойдет на дирижерский пульт,
Пересекая рой поклонов,
Приподымая громкий культ,

[4] Стих А. Блока.
[5] С. И. Танеев, композитор, теоретик музыки и бывший директор Московской Консерватории.
[6] Впоследствии по всей России известный Ф. Трепов.

830 A veil-like spray of muslins
And pink-cream skirt—a murmur;
But a mysterious, rosy fire,
Moving across her countenance
Toward the half-closed dreaminess of lashes,
835 And singeing them with melanite,—
Would sparkle like the northern vistas,
In flippant fan language . . .
Her veil-like shawl is flying
Onto her pink-cream shoulders.

840 And I, a godforsaken Ghibelline,
Prostrate before the Guelfs,—am wordless, goalless:
Her entertaining paladin . . .
She—Raphael's Madonna!
She'd pass,—we'd, flushing, sigh,
845 And idiotically turn weak-kneed . . .
She'd pass with an old, slant-eyed man,
A snub-nosed, hairless eunuch—
She, passing by to take a front row seat,
Laughs thoughtlessly and wordlessly;[4]
850 And all of those electric candles
Would, iridescing, cast their glances
Upon her porcelain shoulders.
And she is thrown a greeting—
A simple one—by Maestro Taneev;[5]
855 The dashing chief of gendarmes[6]
Binocles her from his box seat.

Her eminent high priest,—Safonov:
Would take to the conductor's podium,
Would intersect a swarm of bows,

[4] A verse of Alexander Blok.
[5] S. I. Taneev, composer, theoretician of music and former director of the Moscow Conservatory.
[6] F. Trepov, subsequently renowned throughout Russia.

860 Ее почтенный жрец, — Сафонов:
Кидаясь белой бородой
И кулаками на фаготы, —
Короткий, толстый и седой, —
Он выборматывает что-то;
865 Под люстры палочкой мигнув [7],
Душой, манжетом, фалдой, фраком
И лаком лысины метнув, —
Валторну поздравляет с браком;
И в строгий разговор волторн
870 Фаготы прорицают хором,
Как речь пророческая Норн,
Как каркнувший Вотáнов ворон;
А он, подняв свою ладонь
В речитативы вьолончеля:
875 — «Валторну строгую не тронь:
«Она — Мадонна Рафаэля!»
И после, из седых усов
Надувши пухнущие губы
На флейт перепелиный зов, —
880 Приказ выкидывает в трубы;
И под Васильем Ильичом,
Руководимые Гржимали [8],
Все скрипоканты провизжали,
Поставив ноги калачом.

885 Бесперый прапор подбородком
Попав в просаки — с'кон'апель —
Пройдет по ноткам, как по водкам,
Устами разливая хмель;
Задушен фраком, толст и розов,
890 Ладонью хлопнув в переплеск,

[7] Впоследствии Сафонов дирижировал без палочки.
[8] Гржимали, исполнявший первую скрипку в оркестре, проф. Моск. Консерватории.

860 Inspiring a noisy cult;
    Attacking the bassoons
    With his white beard and fists,—
    Short, fat and hoary-headed,—
    He mutters something to himself;
865 A flick of the baton toward the chandeliers,[7]
    With soul, cuffs, tails, frock coat
    And varnished baldspot all afling,—
    He offers nuptial congratulations to the horn;
    And at the solemn discourse of the horns,
870 Bassoons are prophesying in a chorus,
    Like the prophetic speeches of the Norns,
    Like Wotan's cawing raven;
    And he, having upraised his palm
    To the violoncello's recitativi:
875 —"Don't harm the solemn horn:
    It's—Raphael's Madonna!"
    And later on, out of his whiskers
    Inflating his protruding lips
    Toward the quail-call of the flutes,—
880 He throws an order at the trumpets;
    And under our Vasily Ilich,
    And following Grzhimali's lead,[8]
    The violinicians screech along,
    Their legs tucked tightly, pretzel-like.

885 A greenhorn ensign, having made
    A gaffe—*ce qu'on appelle*—
    Absorbs the notes as he absorbs his vodka,
    Already talking in a drunken jabber;
    Choked by his frock coat, fat and pink
890 Clapping his hands in echo,

[7] Safonov later conducted without a baton.
[8] Grzhimali, concertmaster of the orchestra, was a professor at the Moscow Conservatory.

>   Подтопнув, — лысиной Морозов
>   Надуто лопается в блеск⁹;
>   За ним — в разлив фиоритуры,
>   Бросаясь головой, карга
> 895   Выводит чепчиком фигуры:
>   И чертит *па*, и вертит *туры*
>   Под платьем плисовым нога:
>   Дрожа, дробясь в колоратуры,
>   Играет страстная серьга;
> 900   Пятно все то же щурым ликом
>   На руку нервную легло:
>   Склоняет Скрябин¹⁰ бледным тиком
>   Необъяснимое чело,
>   И — пролетит скрипичным криком
> 905   В рои гностических эмблем,
>   Мигая из пустых эонов;
>   Рукою твердой тему тем
>   За ним выводит из тромбонов
>   Там размахавшийся Сафонов:
> 910   Кидаясь белой бородой
>   И кулаками на фаготы, —
>   Короткий, толстый и немой,
>   Как бы вынюхивает что-то;
>   Присядет, вскинув в воздух нос:
> 915   Вопрос, разнос во взгляде хитром;
>   И стойку сделавши, как пёс,
>   Несется снова над пюпитром;
>   Задохнется и — оборвет,
>   Платком со лба стирает пот;
> 920   И разделяется поклоном
>   Меж первым рядом и балконом.
>
>   И постоит, и помолчит,
>   И по пюпитру постучит:
>   И — все листы перевернулись;

---

⁹ М. А. Морозов, московский меценат того времени (смотри портрет Серова).

¹⁰ Посетитель Симф. Концертов того времени.

      Tapping his feet, Morozov[9] with his baldspot
      Pompously bursts out into sparkle;
      Behind him—in outpourings of fioritura,
      Tossing her head, a hag
895 Draws rhythmic figures with her bonnet:
      She traces *pas* and turns out *tours*
      With leg gambading under velvet dress:
      Vibrating, fracturing into coloratura,
      A passionate earring gambols;
900 Upon a nervous hand a pale face rests,
      As always pinched and wrinkled:
      Scriabin[10] with his nervous tic
      Inclines his inexplicable brow,
      And—would fly by with violin cry
905 Into the swarms of gnostic emblems,
      While winking out of empty eons;
      With steady hand, Safonov, wildly flailing,
      Brings out of the trombones
      The theme of themes:
910 Attacking the bassoons
      With his white beard and fists,—
      Short, fat and taciturn,
      As if he's sniffing something out;
      He'd squat, nose tossed into the air:
915 A question, a berating in sly glances;
      And pointing like a hunting dog,
      He lunges once again above his music stand,
      He gasps and—cuts them off;
      He wipes his forehead with a handkerchief;
920 And he divides himself into a bow
      Between the front row and the balcony.

      He'd stand there and be silent,
      And tap his music stand:
      And—all the pages had been turned;

    [9] M. A. Morozov, Moscow philanthropist of that time (see portrait by Serov).
    [10] Attended the Symphony Concerts at that time.

925 Сердца, как в бой, сердца — рванулись..
И вновь — вскипающая новь;
И вновь — всклокоченная бровь;
И вновь — пройдутся фалды фрака;
И стаю звуков гонит он,
930 Как зайца гончая собака, —
На возникающий тромбон.

Над пухоперою каргою,
Над чепчиком ея счернён
Жеребчиком мышиным — «*он*»,
935 Кто вьется пенною пургою
И льет разменною деньгою,
Кто ночью входит в пёстрый сон
И остро бродит в *ней* — счернён —
Над ней, над нами, над вселенной
940 Из дней, своими снами пленный;
Он — тот, который есть не он,
Кому названье легион:
Двоякий, многоякий, всякий,
Иль просто окончанье, «*Iй*»,
945 Виющийся, старинный змий, —
В свои затягивает хмури,
Свои протягивает дури:
Он — пепелеющая лень
И — тяготеющая тень;
950 Как Мефистофель, всем постылый,
Упорным профилем, как чорт, —
Рассудок, комик свинорылый:
К валторне чёрной он прострт;
Как снег, в овьюженные крыши,
955 Как в мысли, гложущие мыши, —
В мечты, возвышенные свыше, —
Бросает сверженную сушь:
Сухую прописную чушь;

925 The hearts, they leaped, as if to battle . . .
Once more—the seething virgin soil;
Once more—the bushy eyebrow raised;
Once more—the frock coat tails would fly;
And now a flock of sounds he chases,
930 Like hunting hounds a hare,—
Toward the trombone's rising sound.

Above the downy-feathered hag,
Obscured above her bonnet,
A superannuated rake—is "*he*,"
935 Who whirls just like a foamy snowstorm
And spills the coins of his small change,
Who enters motley dreams at night
And acutely ferments in *her*—obscured—
Over him, over us, and over the universe
940 Of the days, a captive of his own dreams;
He is—the one who is not he,
Whose name is legion:
A double, multiple, or universal,
Or just "The Male" itself,
945 A coiling, ancient serpent,—
He draws one to his glooms,
He stretches out his foolishness:
He is—a laziness that turns to ashes,
And—cumbrous shadow figure;
950 Like Mephistopheles, to all repellent,
With stubborn profile, like a devil,—
The mind, a hog-nosed comic actor:
He is outstretched toward the black horn;
As snow at blizzard-ridden roofs,
955 As in a thought those gnawing mice,—
At dreams, uplifted from on high,—
He casts an overthrown aridity:
An arid, trite absurdity;

```
        Упавшим фраком ночь простерши,
960  Кликуши-души, — ходит он —
        Кликуши-души — горше, горше —
        Упавшим фраком — душит: в сон!...


        Черней, упорней гром в валторне:
        Грознее, озорней Она
965  Грозой молниеносной, горней —
        Грозою гор озарена: —


                — Так дымом пепелит и мглеет
                Внеголовый, мгловый слой;
                Как змий, он отдымит ответе
970          В багровом горизонте мглой:
                Слезами облако, светая,
                Слезами полное, молчит;
                И в волны, в воздух — тая, тая, —
                Глазами молнии дрожит,
975          Как воздыханиями арфы,
                Как лепетанием струны —


        Души — Марию зрящей Марфы —
        Из просветленной глубины!..


        И бросят в арфы, — шали, шарфы,
980  Вздыхая раей дорогой, —
        Вон те, Марии, эти Марфы,
        Над жизнью, старою каргой.


        Вы, сестры —


                — (Ты, Любовь — как роза,
                Ты, Вера, — трепетный восторг,
985          Надежда — лепетные слезы,
                София — горний Сведенборг!) —


        Соединив четыре силы
        В троякой были глубиной,
```

        He darks the night with fallen frock coat,
960   The howling souls,—he's walking—
        The howling souls—grief-stricken, bitter—
        With fallen coat—he smothers: into dreams! . . .

        The thunder blacker, more insistent in the horn:
        More threatening and mischievous, She
965   Is illuminated by the lofty lightning—
        The stormy lightning of the mountains:—

            —Like this a Viy-capped, hazy layer
            Turns ashen with the smoke and haze;
            And, like a serpent, will run out of steam, will waft
970   Its haze upon the red horizon:
            With tears, with tears so full,
            The shining cloud is silent;
            And melting, melting—into waves and air,—
            It scintillates with lightning eyes,
975   Like sighings of the harp,
            Like murmurings of the string—

        A heart string—Martha contemplating Mary—
        Out of enlightened depths! . .

        And at the harps they flip,—scarfs, shawls,
980   Sighing with the precious tidings,—
        Those Marys and these Marthas,
        Above our life, that aged hag.

        You, sisters—

            —(You, Charity,—are like a rose,
            You, Faith,—a quivering ecstasy,
985   Hope, you are murmuring tears,
            Sophia—a lofty Swedenborg!)—

        Having united your four forces
        Into a threefold deep reality,

           Меня примите из могилы,
990   Светите оком — Той, Одной, —
           Мечтой вуалевой, как трепет,
           Несущей далевую жизнь
           На опечаленный мой лепет
           Сквозь звуков маревную жизнь.

995   Моя Надежда, дева Отис,
           Милуясь лепетной серьгой,
           Вдыхая цветик, миозотис,
           Из зовов арфы дорогой,
           Бросает взор, лазури-ляпис,
1000   В воздухолетный септакорд:
           И взор, читая звуков запись,
           Над миром —
                        — Аписом —
                                       — простерт!

           Перебегает по ланитам
           В ресниц прищуренную сонь,
1005   Их опаляя меланитом,
           Таимый розовый огонь.

           С неименуемою силой
           С неизреченных аллилуй
           Ко мне, волнуемому Милой,
1010   Мгновенный сеян поцелуй.

           Так из блистающих лазурей
           Глазами полными огня [11],
           Ты запевающею бурей
           Забриллиантилась — в меня:
1015   Из вышины — разгулы света;
           Из глубины — пахнуло тьмой;
           И я был взят из молний лета
           До ужаса — Тобой: Самой!

   [11] Строка Лермонтова «*С глазами полными лазурного огня*» перешла в тему Вл. Соловьева «*Три свидания*», откуда попала в сокращенном виде в мою поэму.

Receive me from the grave,
990 Grant the light of your eye—to Her, the Only One,—
With a dream that quivers like a veil,
Bringing the life of the distances
Through the delusive life of sounds
In answer to my saddened murmuring.

995 Nadezhda mine, the maiden Otis,
Exchanging caresses with her murmuring earrings,
Inhales the flower, miozotis,
From calls of the beloved harp,
And casts her gaze, lapis lazuli,
1000 Into an airborne seventh chord:
Her gaze, reading the sheet of music,
Like Apis—
    —is outstretched—
        —above the world!
That hidden, rosy fire,
Moving across her countenance
1005 Toward the half-closed dreaminess of lashes,
Is singeing them with melanite.

With an unnamable force
Down from unuttered alleluias,
To me, excited by the Dear One,
1010 A momentary kiss is wafted.

Thus from the sparkling azures
With eyes so full of fire,[11]
A storm embarking on its song,
You have begun to diamondize—at me:
1015 Out of the heights—a revelry of light;
Out of the depths—a whiff of darkness;
And I am taken from the summer lightning
O horror—by You: Yourself!

[11] Lermontov's line "With eyes so full of azure fire" became a motif in Vladimir Solovyov's *Three Encounters*, from whence it found its way, in abbreviated form, into my poem.

Ты на меня сходила снами
1020 Из миротворной тишины:
Моей застенчивой весны
Оголубила глубинами;
И мне открылась звуком бурь
Катастрофической цевницы
1025 И милоглазая лазурь,
И поцелуйная денница:
Ее, о время, — опурпурь!

Благонамеренные люди,
Благоразумью отданы:
1030 Не им, не им вздыхать о чуде
Не им — святые ерунды...
О, не летающие! К тверди
Не поднимающие глаз!
Вы — переломанные жерди:
1035 Жалею вас — жалею вас!
Не упадет на ваши бельма
(Где жизни нет — где жизни нет!) —
Не упадет огонь Сент-Эльма
И не обдаст Дамасский свет.
1040 О, ваша совесть так спокойна:
И ваша повесть так ясна:
Так не безумно, так пристойно
Дойти до дна - дойти до дна.
В вас несвершаемые леты
1045 Неутоляемой алчбы —
Неразрывные миголеты
Неотражаемой судьбы...
Жена — в постели; в кухне — повар;
И — положение, и вес;
1050 И положительный ваш говор
Переполняет свод небес:
Так выбивают полотеры
Пустые, пыльные ковры...

To me you have descended in my dreams
1020 Out of the pacifying silence:
You've colored blue the depths
Of this my bashful spring;
And by the sound of storms
And by the catastrophic panpipe,
1025 A lovely-eyed azure was disclosed to me,
And the caressing Morning Star:
O Time,—enpurple it!

The well-intentioned philistines,
Who're steeped in common sense:
1030 It's not for them to sigh for wonders,
It's not for them—this sacred nonsense . . .
Nonfliers! Never elevating
Your eyes to look upon the firmament!
You are—sticks broken into pieces:
1035 I pity you—I pity you!
There'll not descend upon your half-blind eyes
(Where there's no life—where there's no life!)—
There'll not descend St. Elmo's fire,
Damascene light will not blaze forth.
1040 Your conscience is so satisfied;
Your story is so clear:
So decorously, so demurely
To reach the bottom—reach the bottom.
In you unperformable flights
1045 Of insatiable cupidity are—
Indissoluable flash-flights
Of unresisted destiny . . .
The wife—in bed; the cook—in kitchen;
And—status and prestige;
1050 Your optimistic language
Overfills the heavens' vault:
As thus the cleaners beat
Your empty, dust-filled carpets . . .

У вас — потухнувшие взоры...
1055 Для вас и небо — без игры!

. . . .

Мои мистические дали
Смычком взвивались заливным,
Смычком плаксивым и родным —
Смычком профессора Гржимали:
1060 Он под Васильем Ильичом
(Расставив ноги калачом), —
Который, —
         — чаля из эонов
На шар земной, — объятый тьмой,
Рукою твердой на тромбонах
1065 Плывет назад — в Москву, домой:
Слетит, в телодвиженье хитром
Вдруг очутившись над пюпитром,
Поставит точку: оборвет,
Сопит и капли пота льет,
1070 И повернувшись к первой скрипке
Жмет руки и дарит улыбки,
Главой склоняясь в первый ряд,
Где на фарфоровые плечи,
Переливаясь, бросят взгляд,
1075 Все электрические свечи;
Задушен фраком, толст и розов,
Ладонью хлопнув в переплеск,
Бросаясь лысиной, — Морозов
Надуто лопается в блеск.

1080 И вот идет, огней зарнимей
Сама собой озарена,
Неся, как трэн, свое «во-имя»,
Надежда Львовна Зарина;
Вуали — лепетные слезы;

You have—extinguished gazes . . .
1055 Even the sky for you is—playless!
. . . .

My mystic panoramas
Are twirled up by the flowing bow,
The bow both weepy and familiar—
Of Grzhimali's violin:
1060 (His legs tucked tightly, pretzel-like),—
He's under our Vasily Ilich,
Who,—
   —out of eons, steering
Toward the earthly sphere,—engulfed in darkness,
With steady hand on the trombones,
1065 Is sailing back—to Moscow, home:
He'd fly down in a cunning gesture;
Finding himself above a music stand,
He'd make a full stop: cut them off,
And wheeze, and drip with drops of sweat;
1070 And turning to the concertmaster,
He'd shake his hand, distribute smiles,
Bowing his head toward the front row,
Where all of those electric candles
Would, iridescing, cast their glances
1075 Upon those porcelain shoulders;
Choked by his frock coat, fat and pink,
Clapping his hands in echo,
His baldspot lunging out,—Morozov
Pompously bursts out into sparkle.

1080 And here she comes, more lightninglike than fire,
Illuminated from within,
Carrying, like a train, her "in-the-name-of,"—
Nadezhda Lvovna Zarina;
Her veils are—murmuring tears;

1085 Браслеты — трепетный восторг;
Во взорах — горний Сведенборг;
Колье — алмазые морозы:
Блеснет, как северная даль,
В сквозные, веерные речи;
1090 Летит вуалевая шаль
На бледно палевые плечи...

— «Скажи, тобой увлечена
«Надежда Львовна Зарина?»
— «Не знаю я...»

— «Быть может?»
— «Да!»

1095 Выходит музыкантов стая,
И кто-то, фраком отлетая,
В чехол слагает свой кларнет...
Пустеет зал и гаснет свет...

У двери — черные шпалеры;
1100 Стоят: мегеры, кавалеры;
И — ша-ша-ша: шуршат, спеша,
Атласами спускаясь с хоров...
— «Не та калоша: Каллаша! [12]
Стыдливо низится Егоров [13];
1105 Лысеет химик Каблуков — [14]
Проходит в топот каблуков;
Проходит Нос [15] — по воле рока
Он, вы представьте, — без Шенрока!
Выходим!..

[12] Каллаш — московский писатель и критик.
[13] Математик.
[14] Проф. Моск. Университета.
[15] Прас. пов. Нос — посетитель концертов того времени.

1085 Her bracelets—quivering ecstasy;
And in her gazes—lofty Swedenborg;
Her necklace—diamantine frosts:
Would sparkle like the northern vistas,
In flippant fan language;
1090 Her veil-like shawl is flying
Onto her pink-cream shoulders . . .

—"So tell me, have you captivated
Nadezhda Lvovna Zarina?"
—"Don't know . . . "

                —"Might be, perhaps?"
                          —"O yes!"

1095 And the musician flock is exiting,
And someone, frock coat flapping outward,
Inserts his clarinet into its case . . .
The hall is emptying, the lights go out . . .

While at the door—dark queues of people
1100 Are standing: the old hags, the gallants;
And chatter, chatter: they rustle, rushing,
Their satins coming from the balcony . . .
—"Not those galoshes: they're Kallash's"[12]
Egorov[13] sheepishly bends downward;
1105 Professor Kablukov,[14] a balding chemist—
Is passing in a heel stampede;
So, too, is Nos[15]—by the will of fate,
Just think of it, he's—here without Shenrok!
And we go out! . .

[12] Kallash—the Moscow writer and critic.
[13] A mathematician.
[14] Professor of Moscow University.
[15] The barrister Nos—attended the concerts of that time.

4.

　　　　　... Вижу этих дам —
1110　В боа — дородных, благородных;
　　　И — тех: пернатых, страстных дам,
　　　Прекрасных дам в ротондах модных...

　　　Костров каленые столбы
　　　Взовьются в кубовые сини
1115　Из-за редеющей толпы;
　　　Стрекозы, рдеющие в иней,
　　　Метаясь гаснут всем, что есть;
　　　Мордастый кучер прогигикнет;
　　　Снегами радостная весть,
1120　Слетая, сладостно воскликнет;
　　　И прометет — и пронесет
　　　Квадратом лаковым из ночи,
　　　Ударит конским потом в рот,
　　　Завертит огненные очи,
1125　Очертит очерк дорогой
　　　Из соболей в окне кареты...

　　　Вдали слезливою серьгой
　　　Играют газовые светы...

　　　И все, что было, все, что есть —
1130　Снеговерченье ясных далей,
　　　Светомолений светлых весть,
　　　Перелетание спиралей!

　　　Но взвоет улицей зима... —

　　　И быстроногою фигурой,
1135　Из ног выметываясь, тьма
　　　Ростет и сумеречит хмуро
　　　На белобокие дома;

4.

           . . . I see these ladies—
1110 In boas—stout and noble;
      And—others: feathered, ardent ladies,
      Beautiful ladies in their stylish capes . . .

      The red-hot columns of the bonfires
      Whirl up into the indigo-blue sky,
1115 A backdrop to the thinning crowd;
      Dragonflies, glowing into frost,
      Darting, extinguished by everything;
      A fat-faced coachman gee-ups by;
      Through falling snow, Glad Tidings
1120 Would vociferate delightedly;
      The lacquered cube would hurtle by
      Out of the night and rush away;
      It'd hit you in the mouth with equine sweat,
      Would dazzle your fiery eyes,
1125 Would trace the precious outline
      Of sables in the carriage window . . .

      And in the distance, gaslights
      Are playing like the teary earrings . . .

      And all that was, and all that is—
1130 Are snowswirls of the limpid vistas,
      The tidings of my light-prayers,
      The flying back and forth of spirals!

      But winter'd howl along the street . . .—

      And as a quick-paced figure
1135 Uptossing from his feet, the darkness
      Would grow and, lowering, twilightize
      Onto the white-walled houses;

И мнится: темные лемуры,
Немые мимы, — из зимы,
1140 Мигая мимо, строят туры
И зреют речью:
                    — «Ты и мы»!..
Иду, покорный и унылый
Четвероногим двойником:
И — звезденеет дух двукрылый;
1145 И — леденеет косный ком;
Перемерзая и мерцая,
Играя роем хрусталей,
Налью из зеркала лица я
Перезеркаленных лилей, —
1150 И там, под маской, многогрешный,
Всклокочу безысходный срам,
Чтобы из жизни встал кромешный
Безцельный, сумасшедший храм...

Взлетайте выше, злые мимы,
1155 Несясь вдоль крыши снеговой,
Мигая мимо — в зимы, в дымы —
Моей косматой головой!..

О, обступите — люди, люди:
Меня спасите от меня;
1160 Сомкните молнийные груди
Сердцами, полными огня.
Я — зримый — зеркало стремлений,
Гранимый призраком алмаз
Пересеченных преломлений:
1165 Мигнув, отбрасываюсь — в вас,
Как переполненный судьбою
На вас возложенный венец:
Созрею, отдаваясь бою
Родимых, греющих сердец.

It seems to me: dark lemurs,
Mute mimes,—from out of winter,
1140 In flashing past, dance rings
And ripen to a statement:
— "You and we! .
I go, despondent and submissive,
A four-legged Doppelgänger:
And—the two-winged spirit stars out;
1145 And—the inactive lump is icing up;
Congealing and twinkling,
And playing with a swarm of crystals,
I'll pour out of the mirror of my face
Some over-mirrored lilies,—
1150 And there, masked, greatly sinful,
I'll tousle my illimitable shame,
So that from life there would arise the aimless,
Insane temple of outer darkness . . .

Fly higher, evil mimes,
1155 Hurtling like my shaggy head
Along the snowy roof
Flashing past,—into winters, into smoke! . .

O gather round me—crowds of people:
And save me, save me from myself;
1160 Close up your lightninged breasts
With hearts so full of fire.
I'm—visible—a mirror of such striving,
A diamond, spectre-facetted,
Of intersectings of refractions:
1165 Having winked, I recoil—into you,
And overfilled by destiny
With which you have been crowned:
I will mature, and join the battle
Of warming and familiar hearts.

1170 Вы — подойдете, я — омолнен;
Вы — отойдете, я — не тот: —
Я переломлен, переполнен
Переполохами пустот,
Как тени пустолетный конус,
1175 Как облачка высотный лет,
Как бессердечный, вечный тонус
Несуществующих высот.

На тучах строются фигуры:
И я — изъятьем лицевым,
1180 Дробимый, сумеречный, хмурый,
Несусь по кучам снеговым;
Из ног случайного повесы
Тянусь — безвесый, никакой:
Меня выращивают бесы.
1185 Невыразимою тоской...
Мы — неживые, неродные, —
Спирали чьих-то чуждых глаз:
Мы — зеркала переливные —
Играем в ясный пустопляс;
1190 На стенах летом пляшут пятна;
В стакане светом пляшет винт;
И все — так странно непонятно;
И все — какой то лабиринт...
Глаза — в глаза!.. Бирюзовеет...
1195 Меж глаз — меж нас — я воскрешен;
И вестью первою провеет:
Не — ты, не — я!.. Но — мы: но — Он!

А ум, насмешливый, как леший,
Ведет по плоскости иной:
1200 Мы чешем розовые плеши
Под бирюзовою весной;
Перемудрим, перевопросим,
Не переспросим, не поймем,

1170 When you approach me, I am lightninged;
And when you leave, I'm not the same:—
I'm broken in half, filled to the brim
With flarings-up of emptiness,
Just like a shadow's empty-flying cone,
1175 A cloudlet's flight on high,
The heartless and eternal tonus
Of nonexisting heights.

On stormclouds figures are constructed:
And I—with absence of a face,
1180 Fragmented, dour and gloomy,
Dash over the high drifts of snow;
Out of the footsteps of a scapegrace
I stand—I'm weightless, nondescript:
And demons educate me.
1185 With inexpressible anguish . . .
We're not alive, not brothers,—
The spirals of an alien's eyes:
We are—coruscating mirrors—
We play at bright and empty prancing;
1190 The spots prance in summer on the walls;
And in a tumbler a coil of light's aplay;
And all is—oddly unintelligible;
And all is—somehow labyrinthine . . .
Eyes—into eyes! . . A turquoise light is dawning .
1195 Between the eyes—between us—I am resurrected;
The first tidings come wafting:
Not—you, not—I! . . But—we: but—He!

However, wit, derisive, like a woodsprite,
Leads us along a different plane:
1200 We scratch our rosy baldpates
Amid the turquoise spring;
Too clever, we will over-question;
Won't ask again, won't understand;

  Мечту безвременную бросим,
1205 По жизни бременно пройдем;
  И не выносим, и ругаем
  В летах переблиставший дым:
  Бодаем жалобным бугаем [1],
  Брыкаем мерином седым.

1210 Рассудок, свинорылый комик,
  Порою скажет в зовы зорь,
  Что лучше деревянный домик,
  Чем эта каменная хворь;
  И спрячет голову, как страус,
1215 Отскочет в сторону, как пёс,
  Вмаячив безысходный хáос,
  В свой обиходный, злой «*хавóс*»..
  Переварив дары природы
  Тупыми животами,—мы
1220 Перетопатываем годы;
  И—утопатываем в тьмы.

  Вставайте, морочные смены,
  Пустовороты бытия,
  Как пусто лопнувшие пены,—
1225 Да, вас благословляю я!
  Бросай туда, в златое море,
  В мои потопные года—
  Мое рыдающее горе
  Свое сверкающее: «Да»!
1230 Невыразимая Осанна,
  Неотразимая звезда,
  Ты Откровением Иоанна
  Приоткрывалась: навсегда

---

[1] «Бугай»—бык по-малороссийски.

	Surrendering our timeless dream
1205	We pass through life a burden to the earth;
	We can't endure, we curse
	The smoke that sparkled through our years:
	We gore like plaintive bullocks,[1]
	We kick like old grey geldings.
1210	The mind, a hog-nosed comic actor,
	At times will say to sunrise calls
	That a plain cottage would be better
	Than this inert stone ailment;
	It hides its head in ostrich fashion,
1215	And leaps aside like a dog,
	Having incorporated illimitable chaos
	Into its daily, angry *khavós* . . .
	Having digested nature's gifts
	In stupid stomachs,—we
1220	Go tramping, tramping through the years;
	And—tramp away into the darkness.
	Arise, O illusory changes,
	The hollow whirlpools of existence,
	Like bursting empty foam bubbles,—
1225	My benediction be upon you!
	Throw off into the golden sea,
	Into my cataclysmic years—
	My moaning, sobbing grief,
	My luminescent: "Yes"!
1230	My inexpressible Hosannah,
	My irresistible star,
	Through St. John's Revelation
	You've been disclosed to me: forever.

[1] "Bugay"—bull in Ukrainian.

   Кропя духами Аткинсона
1235 Ей ометеленный подъезд,
   Пред Нею, тайною иконой,
   Я упивался блеском звезд;
   Она ко мне сходила снами
   Из миротворной глубины
1240 И голубила глубинами
   Моей застенчивой весны;
   Персты орфической цевницы
   Приоткрывали звуком бурь
   И поцелуйные денницы,
1245 И милоглазую лазурь.

   Остановясь перед киотом,
   Бывало, пав под фонарем,
   Я, полоненный миголетом,
   Моленьем тихим осенен;
1250 В белопокровы, в ветроплясы
   Метясь светелицей на нас,
   Влача свистящие атласы
   Вставал алмазноглазый Спас.
   Бывало: белый переулок
1255 В снегу—дымит; и снег—летит.
   И Богоматерь в переулок
   Слезой перловою глядит.
   Бегу Пречистенкою... Мимо...
   Куда? Мета—заметена,
1260 Но чистотой необъяснимой
   Пустая улица ясна.

   Кто там, всклокоченный шинелью,
   Скрыв озабоченный свой взор,
   Прошел пророческой метелью
1265 (Седою головой—в бобер),
   Взвиваясь в вой седоволосый,
   Своей космою пурговой,

	Aspersing Atkinson's perfume
1235	Upon her snowstormed porch,
	Before Her, my mysterious icon,
	I reveled in the sparkle of the stars;
	To me she has descended in my dreams
	Out of the pacifying depths
1240	And in the depths of this my bashful spring
	She colored all around her blue;
	The fingers of an orphic panpipe
	In sounds of storms disclosed
	Both the caressing morning stars
1245	And also lovely-eyed azure.

	While stopping at an icon grotto,
	Or having kneeled beneath a streetlight,
	I, captivated by a flash-flight,
	Am shadowed over by a quiet prayer;
1250	In the white shrouds, in wind-dances,
	And sweeping toward us with a lamp,
	Dragging his hissing silks and satins,
	The Savior, diamond-eyed, arose.
	And I recall: a white lane—
1255	In haze and smoke; the snow—would fly.
	And down the lane the Blessed Mother
	Is glancing with a pearly teardrop.
	I run along Prechistenka . . . Pass by . . .
	Where to? The traces are—obliterated,
1260	But now the empty lane is bright—
	With pureness inexplicable.

	But who is there, disheveled, in an overcoat,
	Hiding his worried gaze,
	Who passed through this prophetic blizzard
1265	(Into the beaver collar—with his hoary head),
	Up-whirling through the hoary howl
	With shaggy snowstorm mane,

       Снегами сеющий вопросы
       На нас из Вечности самой.
1270   А вихри свистами софистик
       Заклокотали в кругозор
       Взвизжали: «Вот — великий мистик!»
       И усвистали за забор.

       Мигают звезды теософий
1275   Из неба кубового в вой;
       Провеял кризис философий,
       Как некий гейзер снеговой:
       Так в ночи вспыхивает магний,
       Бьет электрический магнит;
1280   И над поклонниками Агни,
       Взлетев, из джунглей заогнит...

       Бегу Пречистенкою — мимо:
       Куда? Мета — заметена;
       Но чистотой необъяснимой
1285   Пустая улица ясна...

       Проснулась на Девичьем Поле
       Знакомым передрогом ширь:

       — «Извозчик: стой»!
                   — «Со мною, что ли»?
       — «В Новодевичий Монастырь»!..
1290   — «Да чтоб тебя: сломаешь сани»!
       . . . .
       И снова зов — знакомых слов:
       — «Там — день свиданий, день восстаний»..
       — «Ты кто»?
                   — «Владимир Соловьев:
       «Воспоминанием и светом»
1295   «Работаю на месте этом»...

And sowing questions through the snows
Upon us from Eternity itself?
1270 But vortices, like hisses of sophistries,
Have boiled up into the horizon,
Have screeched: "Here comes—the mighty mystic!"
And hissed away across the fence.

Stars of theosophies are twinkling
1275 Into a howl out of the dark-blue sky;
The crisis of philosophies has wafted past,
A kind of snowy geyser:
Magnesium thus flashes in the night,
Or an electromagnet pulsates;
1280 And flaring over Agni's worshipers,
The flames rush forth out of the jungles . . .

I run along Prechistenka—pass by:
Where to? The traces are obliterated;
But now the empty lane is bright
1285 With pureness inexplicable . . .

The wide expanses with familiar shiver
Have waked on the Deviche Pole:

—"Hey, coachman: stop!"
                        —"A cab, sir?"
—"Novodevichy Convent! . ."
1290 —"Oh, damn: you'll break the sleigh! . ."
. . . .
And once again the call—of well-known words:
—"Yonder is—the day of encounters, the day of resurrections"
—"And who are you?"
                  —"Vladimir Solovyov:
As recollection and as light
1295 I work at this location . . ."

И — никого: лишь белый гейзер...
Так заливается свирель;
Так на рояли Гольденвейзер
Берет уверенную трель.

1300 Бывало: церковка седая
Неопалимой Купины [2],
В метели белой приседая,
Мигает мне из тишины;
Перед задумчивым киотом —
1305 Неугасимый фонарек;
И упадает легким летом
Под светом розовый снежок.
Неопалимов переулок
Пургой перловою кипит;
1310 И Богоматерь в переулок
Слезой задумчивой глядит.

[2] Церковь Неопалимой Купины в Неопалимовском переулке близ Пречистенки и Девичьего Поля.

       And—no one's there: a mere white geyser . . .
       That's how the reed pipe spouts its tune;
       That's how on the piano Goldenweiser
       Attacks a self-assured trill.

1300 And I recall: the hoary chapel
       Of Neopalimaya Kupina,[2]
       Crouching in the white blizzard,
       Would twinkle at me from the silence;
       Before a pensive icon stand—
1305 An inextinguishable votive light;
       And under it with lightsome flight
       The rosy snowflakes fall away.
       Neopalimov Lane
       Is seething in a pearly blizzard;
1310 And down the lane the Blessed Mother
       Is glancing with a pensive teardrop.

---

[2] The Church of Neopalimaya Kupina on Neopalimov Lane near Prechistenka and Deviche Pole.

ЭПИЛОГ.

Двадцатилетием таимый,
Двадцатилетием чернён,
Я слышу зов многолюбимый
Сегодня, Троицыным днем,—
И под березкой кружевною,
Простертой доброю рукой,
Я смыт вздыхающей волною
В неутихающий покой.

Троицын День и Духов День.

Петроград, 1921 года.

EPILOGUE

      Concealed by twenty years,
      Blackened by twenty years,
      I hear the much-loved call
1315 Today, on Pentecost,—
      Beneath the lacy birch,
      Its kindly arm outstretched,
      I'm washed away by sighing wave
      Into unhushing peace.

          Pentecost and Whitmonday

Petrograd, 1921.

NOTES AND COMMENTS ON THE POEM

The Title

The title of the poem is an echo of "Three Encounters," a long poem by the philosopher Vladimir Solovyov (1853-1900).

The Russian word *svidánie* may be translated into English in four ways: "meeting," "encounter," "rendezvous," and "date." *Svidánie* is related to *vídet'*, "to see." The word implies the sense of vision. The English "meeting" (*vstrécha*) implies both parties are conscious of each other. The English "rendezvous" has a slight erotic undertone, and the word "date" cannot be used, first because the event occurred seventy-five years ago, when there was no such word, and second, the two parties had no agreement to meet. Both English words hint at the double consent of the dramatis personae. "Encounter" has no erotic undertone and does not imply the consent, or even the awareness, of the parties, and therefore is neutral. It has fewer connotations than the other three. And what is even more important, it pertains not only to the poet's first encounter with Zariná but also to the encounter of Bely with the ghost of Vladimir Solovyov. The poet's first love is woven into the contrapuntal fabric of the work, and so is the image of Solovyov encountered by Bely in the home of the philosopher's brother, as a living being, and in the streets of Moscow, as a specter.

The Editions

The poem was written during the Spring of 1921, and was finished on June 20th. Bely lived at that time in Petrograd (renamed Leningrad after 1924). Fragments were published during the work in progress (*Známya*, 1921, no. 2, Berlin) with omissions, errors, and lines later discarded. In 1922, in Petrograd, other fragments appeared (*Zapiski Mechtateley*, no. 5). Bely left Russia in August 1921 (to return in October 1923). Two editions were published: the first in 1921 in Petrograd, by Alkonóst (its owner was Samuil Alyánsky), one of the last publishing houses in private ownership before the printing of all books and periodicals was centralized in the Gosizdat (State Publishing House). This edition (Petrograd, 1921, 70 pages, 3,000 copies) is now a collector's item. It has the mark "R. V. Ts." (i.e. authorized by the Military-Revolutionary censorship). The second edition was published in Berlin in 1922 by the Russian publishing house Slovo. At my request the "Alkonost" edition was taken from the open shelves of Princeton University Library and put in the Rare Book Collection. I consulted it many times, but worked with a Xeroxed copy of the "Slovo" edition inscribed to me by Bely in Berlin on October 6, 1922 ("S ískrennim raspolozhéniem i drúzhboy"). The volume is now in the Beinecke Library at Yale.

The First Encounter was reprinted in the USSR 44 years later in the collection of Bely's verse: *Andrey Bely. Stikhotvoréniya i Poémy*, Biblioteka Poeta (bolshaya seriya). This is the "Poet's Library, Large Series" (there also is a "small series"); Maxim Gorky was its founder, the publishing house "Sovetsky Pisatel" its publisher. The volume is marked "Moskva-Leningrad, 1966," and has 656 pages. The Introduction was written by T. Yu. Khmelnitskaya, the footnotes by N. B. Bank and N. G. Zakharchenko. It was printed in 25,000 copies. In the commentary that follows it will be referred to as *B. B. Poeta*.

The Russian line of the original is indicated on the left margin; if (which is rare) an English line has moved slightly above or below its equivalent Russian line, its number is indicated in brackets following the number of the Russian line. All translations in my text are my own.

PROLOGUE

(1) "Gnome" is associated with the Nibelung mythic dwarfs, the dark forces of the Underworld. Richard Wagner's *Ring des Nibelungen* was well known to Bely, but even more so was the heroic German epic of the thirteenth century. On Wagner and his *Ring*, he wrote in *Arabéski* (p. 142, "Oknó v búdushchee," "A Window into the Future"): "Wagner is only one of the pioneers who announced to us the merging of poetry and music, a merging that inevitably leads to the mystery play . . . although he spoke clumsily in instances where Nietzsche would have bitten off his own tongue."

As Bely's poem "Khristós Voskrés" ("Christ is Risen," 1918) in many ways reminds one of Blok's "Dvenádtsat' " ("The Twelve"), so *First Encounter* sometimes follows Blok's unfinished poem "Vozmézdie" ("Retribution," 1910-21). The image of the gnome was used by Blok in the Prologue to "Vozmézdie":

> Thus Siegfried forges his sword over the fire.
> . . . .
> One stroke—and his faithful Nothung sparkles,
> And Mime, that treacherous dwarf,
> Terror-stricken, falls at his feet.

(Nothung, the sword, is a symbol of the Poet's mission.)

But not only dwarfs and gnomes became very early a recurrent image in Bely's poetry. Giants already in 1899-1900 were an important part of his symbolic system. If dwarfs were mean, cunning, sometimes tame and pitiful, and even comic, the giants were frightful, menacing, and aggressive. The poems numbered 658, 667 (9), and 675 (Malmstad numbering: Ph.D. Dissertation, Princeton, 1969) show the development of the dwarf figure. The Symphonies (1902-8) and especially the later poems show how the image of a giant became, if not a syndrome, an obsession of the poet's.

(5) The Russian word for "stove" is *pech*. Bely uses here a Slavonicism: *peshch*. From Lomonosov (1711-65) to Mayakovsky (1893-1930), every Russian poet made an extensive use of words that have their origin in

NOTES AND COMMENTS

Church Slavonic and gradually became absorbed into and blended with the Russian language. These words give a special coloring to the vocabulary: solemn, ironic, poetic, whimsical, etc., depending, of course, on the syntax and the choice of words that follow and/or precede those Slavonicisms. They were not (and are not) words taken directly from Old Church Slavonic. They came into Russian poetry through the common Slavic language, yet still keep their "ancient" or "old-fashioned" sound. Even the Lord's Prayer has mixed lines of pure Russian and integrated Slavonicisms.

(6-8) This is the first ironic note in the poem, self-debunking and playful.

(10) Here we have the first line rupture, a device Bely liked very much. It has a particularly strong effect in lines 201, 983, and 1002. Later Mayakovsky borrowed this device and used it in the majority of his poems. Both did it for the same two reasons: to give the reader a chance to take a new breath, and to emphasize the interior rhyme or an alliteration.

(11) The Day of the Holy Spirit (see Acts 2:1-4) is the Monday after the end of Pentecost, i.e. Whitsuntide, or the day following Trinity Sunday. In the Russian Orthodox tradition (the same is true in the West) Trinity Sunday comes ten days after the Ascension. On that day, according to the Scriptures, the Holy Spirit descended upon the Apostles gathered in memory of Jesus Christ. The holy day was dedicated to the Holy Spirit to equalize his position with the position of the Father and the Son. In 1921, the Monday after Pentecost was June 20, the day Bely finished his poem. Twenty years before, in 1901, on the day of Holy Spirit, Bely made the decision to become a poet after finishing his "Dramatic Symphony" (in rhythmic prose).

(13-17) In both English and Russian, "tongue" (*yazýk*) may be synonymous with "language"; the image of Pentecostal "tongues of flames" is also common to the two languages.

(16) The word for *gornostáy* is "ermine." It can also be translated as "weasel." Here the image is of the animal rather than the fur.

(18) The bull is an ancient symbol of the celestial Eye, the Creator, the heat and light of the sun, energy, wealth, etc. This is the first symbol in the poem clearly connected with the "Spiritual Science" of Rudolf

Steiner, anthroposophy. The bull is also an attribute of Luke, the Evangelist.

At the time Bely wrote his poem he was an anthroposophist, and was longing to get out of Russia and go back to Switzerland, where Rudolf Steiner, the high priest of the sect, lived and worked. Steiner (1861-1925) was on a lecture tour of Europe before World War I when Bely met him. According to Steiner's teaching, man is the center and goal of the universe. He acknowledged the spiritual progress of mankind and created his own pragmatic values. His philosophy was (and is) mainly a method of thinking. He accepts karma of the Hindu religion, and the redeeming of man in subsequent reincarnations. His "Spiritual Science," as he called it, is "occultism for the West," and it relates Eastern religions to Christianity.

(19) Lion, Leo—symbol of action, authority, ferocity, the mind, reason, nobility, pride, vigilance, and the spirit of life. The lion is an attribute of Mark, the Evangelist.

(20) The Russian word *milot'*, very seldom used, means the traditional vestment of John the Baptist (lambskin).

(21) The eagle—symbol of ascension, freedom, immortality, majesty, power, faith, fearlessness, virtue, etc. The eagle is the attribute of John, the Evangelist and presumed author of the Apocalypse.

(23) Bely plays with the initials of Jesus: in German, Jesus Christus would be *ICH* (first person singular); in Russian the *I* and the *X* (pronounced as English *KH*) when superimposed would result in the Russian letter Ж (zh) and suggest the word *zhizn'* ("life"). I was present once when Bely tried to explain these occult intricacies to a couple of skeptics, and the poet Vladislav Khodasevich (1886-1939) wanted to know how all this would sound and look in Italian, French, and Spanish. Bely was at a loss to answer these questions.

The image of Christ, the Savior, the Crucified, haunted Bely from his youth. He identified himself with Christ in his poetry, and in his last public speech before leaving Western Europe for the Soviet Union he again went back to that figure (see my autobiography *The Italics Are Mine*, New York, 1969, pp. 165-66). Sometimes this identification seemed to be a compulsive idea, and reminded one of Friedrich Nietzsche's *Ecce Homo*.

(25) The Russian word *bogoslóv* ("theologian") is also a combination of the two words "God" and "word." Here it applies to the Apostle John, author of the Fourth Gospel, three Epistles, and the Book of Revelation (Apocalypse).

(27) Bely mentions three Evangelists whose attributes are the Angel, the Lion, and the Eagle. Luke has been left out, but his attribute has been mentioned on line 18.

(32) Sacred fire is represented in Hindu philosophy by Agni, one of the three chief deities of the Vedas—Agni (Sanskrit); Ignis (Latin); Ogon' (Russian). Agni's votaries appear in lines 636 and 1280.

1.

(36) First love—Margaríta Kiríllovna Morózova (1873-1958), a famous Moscow beauty (see her portrait by Valentine Serov) and wife of a well-known Moscow businessman, millionaire, Maecenas, and owner of the Publishing House "Put' " (The Path), Mikhail A. Morózov. In their mansion in Moscow, poets, painters, and composers gathered: Scriabin played, Alexander Blok read his verse, and many others were frequent guests. It was one of the sumptuous "salons" of the Symbolist period. Bely at first corresponded with Morózova, not personally knowing her. Only in 1905 was he introduced to her and did he become a guest at her evening parties. At that time he was already involved with Lyubov Blok, the wife of the poet.

(38) "Darknesses" is one of many unusual and unused plurals that Bely liked so much.

(39) The war—the First World War of 1914-18.

(43) Swallows have a long tradition in Russian poetry; among others, Derzhavin, Fet, Khodasevich, and Mandelstam wrote poems on swallows. European Russia has no exotic birds, and the fast-flying, sky- and water-loving swallow has a symbolic connotation for Russian poets. Its swiftness and nearness to man (it nestles under the roof) give it a special character, somehow placing it midway between other birds and angels.

(50) There are some light overtones of parody on Pushkin's verse—specifically on *Eugene Onegin*—in this line. And again we are able to detect it in line 1021, and in lines 838-39, repeated in lines 1090-91 at the

end of the poem. Bely certainly did not do it deliberately but, rereading his draft, he could not but notice what he wrote; he liked it and did not cross it out.

(53) *Zaryá* in Russian means sunrise and also sunset ("One *zaryá* hastens to replace another / Granting the night a half-hour" said Pushkin about the white nights). In Bely's as in Blok's verse, *zaryá* is always sunrise, except when they both specify it as the evening. The years 1898-1900 were meaningful to both poets, and the most important image of these years was the "dawn," which could be understood on three levels: their personal maturing (they both were born in 1880); the destiny of Russia in the approaching new century; the dawn of a new epoch for the world. It was "the era of the dawns" says Bely in his memoirs. "Do you remember the first love / And the dawns, the dawns, the dawns?" wrote Blok in a poem in 1909. Bely spoke about it reminiscing: "In 1900-1 we, the young ones of the era, were hearing something like sounds and noises and seeing something like lights. . . . It was not a dream, it was the feeling of a real fact." He names two authors who had a tremendous impact on him, Vladimir Solovyov and Nietzsche, and two composers, Beethoven and Schumann. "We, the young ones, felt the physiological fact of the dawn. . . . The spring of 1901 it seems was full of eschatological premonitions" (*Vospominániia o A. A. Bloke*, repr. from *Epopeía*, Munich, W. Fink, 1969, pp. 1-4).

(55) William Holman Hunt (1827-1910), whom Bely spells "Golber Gent," was the Pre-Raphaelite painter, friend of the Rossettis, a member of the Pre-Raphaelite Brotherhood, and author of *Pre-Raphaelitism and the Pre-Raphaelite Brotherhood* (1905). (The edition of *B. B. Poeta* 1966 repeats the erroneous spelling.) There was a compulsive need in Bely, an unconscious urge, to distort names: he spoke of *Geist*bergstrasse (where Khodasevich and I lived in 1922) although it was *Geiss*bergstrasse. But *t* was there to remind everybody of the word *Geist* ("spirit") and give the street a meaning.

(57) The students of the universities in Russia before 1917 had to wear a uniform: a long frock coat of dark green cloth with white edging, a semimilitary cap of the same colors, and white gloves.

(61) Maya—in Hindu religious philosophy—the Veil of the World. Also: illusion personified as a female form, and the transparent curtain that covers the universe.

(62) Cotillion (from the French)—a quadrille in which are inserted other dances, such as the waltz, the polka, and the mazurka.

(63) Face powder and Creme Simon were famous French cosmetics, still used in the 1930s.

(64) Atkinson—English perfume manufacturer. Atkinson's "White Rose" was the most elegant scent at the beginning of the century.

(65) Upanishads—ancient philosophic and theosophic writings of the Hindus of the Veda period (seventh and sixth centuries B.C.), commenting on the Vedas in poetic dialogues. These were written in Sanskrit and "revealing the Word." Partial Russian translations started appearing circa 1900.

(66) Anupadaka—probably Anutadaka (Sanskrit). According to the theosophists, one of the seven worlds (or spheres), also called Monadic (one of the two highest levels among the seven). Anutadaka is not yet accessible to any human. The Monad is a part of the Logos and therefore has also three aspects: wisdom, will, and activity.

(69) Ananda—one of the names of Siva meaning "Joy-Happiness." Bely's footnote is mistaken.

(71) Dhainand—probably Dhainan, "Conqueror of the Riches," a title of Arjune (Hindu god). This name was adopted by the nineteenth-century preacher of Hindu religion, Swami Sarasvati Dhainan.

(72) Darmotarra—probably Damodara, one of the names of Krishna, literally meaning "Tied by a rope across his belly." Also used as a name by a commentator and philosopher of India, Darmakirti. Bely, again, has made a mistake in his footnote.

(75) Dimitry Ivanovich Mendeléev (1834-1907), Russian chemist, professor of Petersburg University, inventor of the Periodic System of classification of elements; also father of Lyubov and father-in-law of Alexander Blok.

(78) Robert Boyle (1627-91), British chemist and physicist.

(78) Johannes Diderik van der Waals (1837-1923), Dutch physicist.

(81-82) There is here a touch of parody of some of Lomonosov's odes.

(99, 108-9, 114-18) This is a spoof on the "deterministic generation" of "fathers" of this era. Bely used the myth of Zeus descending upon Leda (or Europa, or Semele, or some other mythical female figure). The trident here has a strong symbolic meaning, and there is a beautiful and at the same time comic sound effect in the original Russian: *bogovbelogolovy*.

(123) Ivan Mikhailovich Grevs (1860-1941), professor of history, famous medievalist (in his time) at Petersburg University. In Russian, *Grevs* rhymes with *Zevs* ("Zeus").

(125) Valery Yakovlevich Bryusov (1873-1924), poet-Symbolist, a great figure in Moscow between 1895 and 1916. Bely's neologism making a verb out of a noun ("hell") pertains to Bryusov's connection with black magic (see his novel *The Fiery Angel* about witchcraft).

(126) Hades, or Aides—land of roots, Kingdom of Darkness, Greek underworld, and at the same time—the King of this realm, the son of Kronos and brother of Zeus, Hades-Pluto. The underworld was guarded by many-headed Cerberus and surrounded by the river Styx. The pun is: *gádost'/Gadés*, where *gádost'* means "dirty trick."

(137) The crescent moon has horns, an endearing notion from fairy tales. The horns do not look like horns of a wild beast but like antlers of a fallow-deer. Bely used this image to explain his concept of metaphor in *Simvolizm* (1910, pp. 445-8): "The horn is sharp and white, the moon is sharp and white. The moon like a white sharp horn, the horn like a white sharp moon (simile). The white-horned moon—a comparison, and finally—the moon, the white horn, a metaphor."

The horn as something sharp and piercing has always been a recurrent image in Bely's poetry. From here we go to all piercing things: a needle, a sword, a hatpin, the horn of a rhinoceros piercing the body of a philosopher, and more. And Apollon Apollonovich Ableukhov, the Senator in Bely's novel *St. Petersburg*, has on his coat of arms "a unicorn perforating [sic!] a knight."

(138) The Russian verb *topýrit'* ("protrude," "extend") is used in an unusual prefixed form of the imperative.

(139) The Russian word *vzórich*, a patronimic or family name, is Bely's neologism. It comes from *vzor*—the way one is looking at something. Making it sound like the person who is looking at something, giving it the masculine gender (in Russian, the moon is masculine gender if it is *mésyats* and feminine if it is *luná*) adds to the line the benefit of a trope—personification, of course.

(140) And the moon as a body hanged in the skies is again a successful personification.

(142) *Ledyn'* is an allusion to the hanged one: the frustrated skies; or, maybe, the whole icy firmament.

(154) "The forest of symbols" is that line of Baudelaire that started the whole Symbolist movement: "La Nature est un temple. . . ./ L'homme y passe a travers des forets de symboles . . . " The expression *zelióny shum* ("green noise") was coined by the poet N. Nekrasov (1821-78).

(167) To illustrate the nonsense of which this pun has been built, the endings of two lines should be transliterated:

> *baldý boltáya* (gerund ending of the verb *boltát'*)
> *darvaldáya* (genitive of a noun, masculine, singular).

They both have a strong onomatopoeic effect. The rhyme is funny, the sound effect comic; the sense—nonexistent. And somewhere lurking in the background is sheer playfulness. The word cluster *darvaldáya* derives from a line by a minor poet of the nineteenth century, Fyodor Glinka (1786-1880), "The Dream of a Russian in a Foreign Land" (*Son rússkogo na chuzhbíne*). Lines 25-28 follow in English translation:

> Rushes along the lively troika,
> Along the highway, to Kazan',
> Under the shaft-bow swings and jingles
> The bell, the gift of my Valday.

(172) Letaev, "my father," "the professor," "the dean," is a character in *Kotik Letaev*, Bely's autobiographical novel written in 1915-16 (English translation by Gerald Janeček, Ardis, Ann Arbor, 1971), and from an unfinished one: *The Crime of Nikolai Letaev* (1921-22) partially published in two periodicals and later reworked as *The Christened Chinaman* (or *Baptized Chinaman*) and published in 1927. In some details the father figure in these novels also reminds us of Ableukhov, the old Senator from *Petersburg*—ugly, old, distraught, cold, preoccupied with remote matters, inhuman, and unloved. This was Professor Nikolai Vasilyevich Bugáev, famous mathematician and Dean of Moscow University, with whom his son apparently could not communicate.

(189) Nikolai Alekseevich Úmov (1846-1915), professor of physics at Moscow University.

(191) To convey a solemn (and utterly comic) picture, Bely puts the words "hair" and "neck" in Church Slavonic.

(192) James Clerk Maxwell (1831-79) the great Scottish physicist, professor of physics, author of *Electricity and Magnetism* (1873), inter alia.

(195) Sir Joseph John Thomson (1856-1940), the great English physicist, discoverer of electrons and later (1906) the recipient of the Nobel Prize in Physics. He became famous after writing his treatise on vortex rings and atomic structures. In 1893 appeared his *Notes on Recent Researches in Electricity and Magnetism*.

(201) Friedrich Nietzsche (1844-1900). One of the foremost authors read by Russian Symbolists of Bely's generation. The first articles about his work appeared in Russia in 1892-93 in the periodical *Problems of Philosophy and Psychology* (by Preobrazhensky, Grot, Lopatin, and Astafiev). The memoirs of Lou Andreas-Salomé appeared translated into Russian in the *Northern Messenger* (*Severny Vestnik*) in 1896. The rhyme is ironic: Nietzsche rhymes with *prýtche*, which is a comparative form of the adjective "nimble."

(202) Pierre Curie (1859-1906), the French chemist. This is the place to mention the words that Bely selected when speaking of scientists: darkness, paradox, explosions, storms, forces, dynamite, bombs, atomic bomb; and also—to destroy, to burst, blow up, fly up, split.

(206) "Son of Ether" is reminiscent of Lermontov's "Demon":

> I, the free Son of Ether,
> I will take you to realms beyond the stars.

(211) [212]. The Russian word *vzvoy* (a spray that bursts with a whirl) does not exist as a noun; this is a neologism that Bely coined. The pattern would be: *vít'sya* (infinitive) and *vzvít'sya* (infinitive), and the action of this verb would be *vzvoy*. But it also has a strong implication of "howl" (*voy*), which makes an oxymoron applied to the rushing fire.

(216) The pun is made from two words: *bézdna* ("abyss") and *bez dna* ("with no bottom"). Nabokov played with these words in *The Gift*, saying that the last tzar somehow reigned between Bézdna (a railroad station where a bomb explosion was meant to kill Alexander III, father of Nicholas II) and another railroad station, Dno ("bottom"), where Nicholas was forced to sign his abdication.

(218) Dalai Lama—high priest of Buddhist religion, has also power over the civil laws. He is chosen at his birth. There is a sound effect in the Russian lines: *Dalailamamolodóy—belogolóvykh Gimaláev*.

(230) Lazulite—a crystalline azure-blue mineral.

(230-31) These two lines are examples of Bely's fondness for mixing one- or two-syllable words with four- or five-syllable words, and this in Russian, because of the words' accent, gives a purely musical effect.

(231) Melanite—black garnet.

(236-37) Two telescoped adjectives (twice) to form two synesthesiae: *Zelenosládkie—zelenogór'kie* ("greensweet"—"greenbitter").

(240-41) Tigers symbolize beauty, cruelty, cunning, grace, greed, and strength. In Greek mythology they are connected with Dionysus: he dressed in tiger skin, he rode a tiger alone and with Ariadne, he came back from India on a tiger, he transformed himself into a tiger.

(256) Bely blends two words in one: *dukh* ("aroma," "fragrance," and also "spirit"); and *véyat'* ("to wave," "to blow"). Out of one noun and one verb he makes one present, active participle. This is the first composite word created by Bely, the second comes in line 259: *tyomnolónny* from *tyómny* and *lóno* ("dark" and "womb"). There will be scores of them later: composite verbs, adjectives, nouns, participles, and adverbs. They will be pointed out in this commentary.

(258) Bely spells *Zaratustr*: the correct spelling is *Zaratustra*. He makes a blend of Zarathustra and Zoroastr. The second name is a Greek distortion of the name of the Persian philosopher of the seventh century B.C. Nietzsche's *Thus Spoke Zarathustra* was translated into Russian in the late 1890s. The *Complete Works of Friedrich Nietzsche* were announced "in four volumes," but the publication was discontinued. In 1900-3, nine volumes were published. The expression "streams of the word Zaratustr" could have two meanings: in the first, Bely is speaking of Nietzsche's work and the title of his book; in the second, Bely speaks about the name per se, the sound of the Iranian philosopher's name, especially the ending *tustr* that echoes the Russian word of "streams" (*strúi*). The Alkonost edition has a misprint: *strun* instead of *strúi*.

(262) In Russian (using the instrumental case) one may say instead of music of Beethoven, or Beethoven's music, *zvuchít Beethovenom* ("re-

sounds with Beethoven" without the preposition), which is a metonymy.

(263) The Noblemen's Club, or the Noblemen's Assembly Hall, was a concert hall. The building still exists: it stands on the corner of Bolshaya Dmitrovka and Okhotny Ryad.

2.

(271) *Stezyá* is "path" (fem.). Bely makes it *stez'*. He is using an archaic form (as in *pésnya—pesn'*, or *básnya—basn'*) and makes the word sound unusual. To make a word new or strange would be his first consideration. The rhyme would be only the second consideration.

(273) *Vzreváet* ("matures," "ripens") derives from *zret', sozrevát*. A neologism is formed, whimsical and strong, suggesting human warmth, which gives a beginning, not an end, to the ripening of ideas, the start of a thinking process.

(275) Here a participle is formed (*lepestyáshchikh*) out of a noun via an invented verb. The word *tsvet* usually means "color." Bely uses the word in its second meaning, rarely used, which is "flower" (*tsvetók*). But no misunderstanding arises.

(276) [274] The adjectives ending in *-istaya* (fem.) or *-ísty* (masc.) or *-ístoe* (n.) imply a less strong quality than the conventional endings *-yi*, *-aya*, *-oye* make them. Here the word "snowy" has less emphasis than the ordinary *snézhnaya* would have.

(281) Mikhail Sergeevich Solovyov, the younger brother of the philosopher Vladimir Solovyov. Both were sons of the historian S. M. Solovyov and brothers of Vsevold Solovyov, a writer of popular historical novels. Vladimir Sergeevich Solovyov (1853-1900) was one of the main influences on Russian Symbolism, although he never accepted either Balmont or Bryusov, and ironically dismissed them by writing parodies on their verse and not recognizing in the younger generation his devoted followers. He is one of the principal characters in *The First Encounter*, and reading it we realize that in these fateful years, charged with premonitions of "dawn," Bely's days and nights were spent mostly at the apartment of Mikhail and at the grave of Vladimir. Bely's thinking was permeated with the image of the Eternal Feminine from the poems of the

philosopher, his deep interest in Christian Symbolism and the personality of Christ, his ideas of ecumenism and the Universal Church, and the doctrine of Wisdom as Sofia which played so large a part in the formation of Bely's thought and no less in that of Alexander Blok. In his memoirs (first version 1921-23), Bely tried to connect the philosophical ideas of Vladimir Solovyov with the "Spiritual Science" of Rudolf Steiner. Bely wrote: "Transmuting logic into Christology and transmuting nature into Cosmos-Sofia Solovyov unconsciously posited a purely anthroposophic theme, because the meeting of Cosmos-Sofia and Logos-Christ is a confrontation between the emotional and spiritual bases of human consciousness" (*Vospominaniia o A. A. Bloke*, p. 36).

(288) The neologism *zolotokhókhloy* ("golden-tufted"), later repeated twice and connected as much with the hair as with the beard of Mikhail Solovyov, has a lovely sound and a playful meaning.

(294) Bely was nineteen years old in the year 1899.

(300) In French and English the word is "bistre" and means dark beige or light brown. This was the fashionable color of the drawing rooms of the *fin de siècle* (together with pale green). Bely misspelled the word as *biskr* and put it in quotation marks.

(301) Foreign words accepted and incorporated into the Russian language (like *pal'tó, pensné, turbó*), all of neuter gender, are not declined and not to be tampered with, but Bely forms an adjective that in the context sounds witty and right: the pattern is the same as in *linéynyi* or *eléinyi*. The shining lens of the pince-nez is said to be *pensnéynoe*.

(306) The "blue" eyes of Mikhail Solovyov are looking at Bely. And what does he do looking at the poet? He (and the adjective is blended with the noun) *goluboglázit*. *Golubóy* is "blue," *glaz* is "eye."

(318) *Rózblesk* is a neologism. The word is *blesk* ("sparkle"), and *roz* is a prefix.

(324) Thomas Aquinas (1225?-74)—Scholastic philosopher, the Angelic Doctor (Doctor Angelicus), he entered the Dominican Order and was canonized by Pope John XXII; a systematizer of Catholic theology, and author of philosophical system known as Thomism.

(332) Vladimir Solovyov was at this time (1899-1900) alive. Bely saw him a couple of times in Mikhail's apartment, and once—in a Moscow

street, at night—in a snowstorm. His name in the poem fits in the line, forming two iambics and one pyrrhic: ¯ ´ ¯ ¯ ¯ ´.

(335) The Russian word *purgovóy* (sing.) and *purgovýe* (plur.) seems to be unstable in its stress: Bely stresses it on its second syllable, Blok in "The Twelve" puts the stress on the third syllable; Bely himself, on line 406 puts the accent on the third syllable.

(336) *"Na vek odnó"*—(forever One) is charged with meaning given it by Vladimir Solovyov in his poem *Známenie* ("The Sign"),—see p. 174 of Solovyov's collection of poems, *Stikhotvoreniia*, Moscow, 1915. Here is an English translation of the poem:

> The One, forever One! Let through the dark slumbering Temple
> Flash the hellish light and the thunder quash the silence!
> Let everything crumble—one banner will never flinch!
> One shield will never move from the destroyed wall!
> In awakened terror we ran at the sacred place,
> Our Temple was filled with suffocating fumes,
> Broken silver shreds were scattered around,
> And black smoke clung to the torn rugs.
> But the sign of the Immaculate Behest was in its place,
> Bathed by light between heaven and earth, and the same light
> That poured on the Maiden of Nazareth came in front of her
> Illuminating the vainglorious poison of the Snake.

Bely did not know Yeats, at least not in 1921, and his beautiful line, "Trembling of the veil of the Temple."

(340) The ambers are here treated as if they were metal, liquid-smelted.

(349) O. M. is the wife of Mikhail Sergeevich, Olga Mikháilovna. The marriage was a happy one: he was immersed in his brother's and his own literary work, and became after the death of Vladimir his spiritual heir and the editor of his complete works; she translated modern French literature and was hostess to many Moscow academic and literary personalities. In January 1903 Mikhail died after an illness, and Olga the same night committed suicide, leaving their only son Sergei Mikhailovich an orphan. He was at that time 17 years old.

(353) Chetí-Minéi—books of religious readings (circa ninth century) from Byzantium, arranged for every day of the month, with descriptions

of the lives of saints, legends, sermons, and apocrypha. These were didactic and imitated the style of the *Acta Sanctorum*. Until the middle of the nineteenth century these books were the basic Sunday readings in Russian Orthodox middle class families. Olga Mikhailovna, although a devotee of the French "decadents," apparently got a special pleasure from these "sacred" books.

(354)   Alfred de Vigny (1797-1863), French poet and author of the historical novel *Cinq-Mars*. Bryusov translated and edited his work in 1909.

(356)   *Carmen*—a novella by Prosper Merimée and the opera by Bizet. This work of Merimée was widely admired in Russia from the year it appeared (1845); the opera was a great success from its first performance to the present. See the cycle of Blok's poems, *Carmen*.

(356)   Jules Barbey d'Aurevilly (1808-89). Author of "Les diaboliques," *Le Chevalier des Touches*, and others, a romantic and an early "decadent," widely read in his time.

(358)   Álya—the mother of the poet Alexander Blok, Alexandra Andreevna (1860-1923). She divorced the poet's father, a professor of political science (who wrote the first article on Karl Marx in Russian) at Warsaw University, Alexander L'vovich Blok, and later married Colonel Kublítsky-Piótukh. She was the daughter of the well-known professor of Petersburg University, Andrey Beketov. The grandmother of Blok and his aunts all were emancipated women, busy demanding women's rights, translating Balzac and the Goncourt brothers; they were distant cousins (by marriage) of Olga Solovyov.

(362)   The long, involved, and fascinating story of the friendship of two greatest poets of Russia of the twentieth century has been told and discussed in a score of books, memoirs, articles, and biographies. From calling each other "brothers" to planning a duel, avoided only by a miracle; from coldness to tenderness; and from harmony to strong disagreement, they both went through a dramatic relationship in the 15 years of their mutual careers. Blok was born the same year as Bely (1880) and died in 1921 (this is when I first saw Bely, who was one of the pallbearers at Blok's funeral). There is (until 1921) a parallel in their lives; they had identical feelings toward most of the issues of their time: the First World War, the February Revolution, the October Revolution, the end of Symbolism as a literary trend, the rise of Mayakovsky. Their personal

attraction to each other and devotion was marred at one time by Bely's infatuation with Lyubov Blok, the wife of the poet. Blok and Bely often irritated each other, but forgave each other every offense—as romantic poets did a hundred years before them. Bely had a tremendous admiration for Blok's work. His recollections, which later grew into an epic of the first quarter of our century, bear witness to this. Their correspondence began in 1903, before the two poets actually met. At that time Blok already had written his "Ante Lucem" poems (1898-1900), whose title meant the *zóri*, about which Bely was also writing at that time.

(364) Sergei Mikhailovich Solovyov (1885-1942), son of Mikhail and Olga and nephew of Vladimir. First an infant prodigy, then a minor poet, later an Orthodox priest, a translator. He was married to the sister of Bely's first wife (Asya Turgeneva), and barely survived during Stalin's time.

(367) Sergéi Nikoláevich Trubetskóy (1863-1905), professor of philosophy, member of the Liberal Party, head (*rektor*) of Moscow University. Bely was a student of his.

(370) At one time Lyubov Blok was connected with the image (in the work of Blok as well) of the "Maiden of the Rainbow Gate."

(372) The turquoise call (*biryuzóvy zov*)—a synesthesia.

(379) The number of Solovyov's relatives was, indeed, great. And among them, apart from those already mentioned, was the aunt, the sister of Vladimir and Mikhail, Polikséna (1867-1924), a poet and translator, a friend of Zinaida Gippius, the editor of a progressive children's magazine. Like her illustrious brother Vladimir, she never married. Among her translations was the first Russian translation of Lewis Carroll's *Alice's Adventures in Wonderland*.

(388) *Bogoslóv*—an appellation for Saint Gregory, as well as for Saint John. This is Gregory Nazianzus, a fourth-century theologian.

(392) The plural applied to the Russian word for "Latin" is without tradition and pattern, but not out of place here.

(396) Sonya N. The footnote in the 1966 Soviet edition, *B. B. Poeta*, gives the following information: this is Sofya Giatsíntova, born in 1895 (which is obviously a mistake: she could not then have been five years old at the time Seryozha was in love with her). She was an actress in her later

years. Why Bely gives her a last name starting with the capital letter *N* when it really starts with *G* is not explained.

(397) The Russian word *klóchen'* comes from *klok*, "a tuft" (of hair).

(399) Nadezhda is a common Russian name. She, Vera, and Lyubov, according to legend, were three daughters of St. Sophia. The name of the mother means "wisdom," Vera means "faith," Nadezhda—"hope," and Lyubov—"love" (corresponding to English "Charity"). The patronymic *L'vovna* comes from the name Lev, Leo. This homonym also means the sign of Leo and lion. Zarina derives, of course, from *zaryá*—the dawn of the beginning of the century.

(401) The adjective "mysterious" becomes a noun, "the Mysterious One," a transformation that happens sometimes (and not so seldom) in the Russian language.

(405-27) Solovyov's concept clearly applied here to Bely's first love: she is the embodiment of Wisdom (Sophia), and the daughter of Leo, who is the Lion of Judah's tribe, perhaps the Messiah himself. See Gen. 49:9, and Rev. 5:5.

(417) The Alkonost edition has a misprint in line 417: the word should not be divided by a hyphen.

(431) Serapis is an Egyptian god combining attributes of Osiris and Apis, who was a sacred bull worshiped by the ancient Egyptians.

(441) Arbat—the great thoroughfare going from the center of Moscow to the Ring of the Sadovayas. It connects "downtown" Moscow (Vozdvízhenka, Známenka, etc.) with Smolénsky Market and the periphery. This was the center of Moscow's "Chelsea" or "Greenwich Village," the district mostly populated by the artists and intellectuals.

(448) Strictly speaking, *zýbka* is something that can be swayed or rocked: a cradle, or a seesaw. Here it is lightly and rhythmically rippling water.

(453) Brahma—god the creator in the Hindu divine triad.

(462) In 1922 on one of the corners of Arbat there could still be seen the old signboard with green faded lettering over the old stationery store. (Khodasevich pointed it out to me.)

(468) According to Bely, Vladimir Solovyov was distinguished by:

shaggy hair, enormous height, a cloak, a fur hat, a beaver collar, huge eyes, and fiery talk. D. S. Merezhkovsky used to say that Solovyov scared him with his unique thunderous laugh, which was as frightening as it was unpleasant.

(471) *Ledyn'* in Russian means an icy space or glacier. Here it is accompanied by the adjective "interplanetary." (See line 142.)

(472) Noncanonic plural *síni* (plural of *sin'*) is coined by Bely. It has a connotation of the "essence of blue."

(475) Devíche Póle—an open space (at that time) beyond the Zubovsky Boulevard leading to the Clinics of the Faculty of Medicine, and further on to the Novodevichy Convent (in the far southwest corner of Moscow). *Devíche Pole* could be translated as "Maiden Field," and, indeed, the old German Baedeker calls it "Jüngferfeld."

(477) The verb *vólim* (inf. *vólit'*), "to will," is a neologism. (See also line 710.)

(482) Two adjectives blend into one—a frequent occurrence. *Zolotokáryaya* (gold-brown) has, as all Russian words do, only one stress.

(484) "Mystic" (or even metaphysical) gossip is a part of Symbolist jargon.

(487) Voanerges or Boanerges is misprinted here as *Voamerges*. In the 1966 *B. B. Poeta* version, this has been corrected. Jesus Christ gave this name to John and James Zebedee, two of his Apostles. It means "Sons of Thunder." See Mark 3:17.

(488) John the Divine, the presumed author of the Apocalypse.

(490) The Novodevichy Convent built in 1524. Peter the Great forced his sister (the legal heir to the throne) to take the veil, and she stayed there as a prisoner till she died. Napoleon visited it in 1812.

(492) *Zlatozór* is a coined word suggesting a fairy tale cupola or a transparent building, looking toward dawn, shimmering with gold. Or, perhaps, a king who sits under such a cupola.

(493) Amianthus—a very fine and silky asbestos.

(495) The verb "to become like turquoise" (*biriuzét*) is coined by Bely. He is using here its participle. The pattern of it is the same as in the Russian words "to become red" (*krasnét'*) or "to become black" (*chernét'*).

(495) The "light-weight pond" is a synesthesia.

(502) The word *vózdukh* is a homonym: first meaning is obvious, it is "air." The second meaning is used very seldom, and the contemporary dictionaries do not mention it. This is the cover on the chalice, where the Sacrament is kept. In the Russian (Eastern Christian) tradition during the mass the Sacrament (bread and wine) is brought out of the Altar by the priest and given to the communicants. The chalice is covered by a velvet napkin (usually red), richly embroidered in gold. It covers the chalice entirely and is taken off before the communion starts.

(511) The word *óblako* means "cloud." It is neuter, but Bely, and before him Blok, liked to use it in its masculine form: not *óblako* but *óblak*:

> The violin started singing, and an airless cloud
> Arose between us. And nightingales
> Filled our dreams. . . .
> (A. Blok, *Complete Works*, 1960, vol. 3, p. 217)

(513) *Izmléy*, imperative of the verb *izmlét'* ("abate"). Never used before and strictly speaking existing only in the form *somlét'*. The imperfective aspect is *mlet'*.

(516) This is a paraphrase from the prayer for the dead.

(522) This is not, as one might think, derived from the verb *klyánchit'* ("to beg"). The wreaths of the cemetery have nothing to beg from the passers-by. This is an onomatopoea, and the sound of the word *klyánch* to the Russian ear gives the image of porcelain flowers on a cross, swaying back and forth in the wind.

(532) *Tsvet* and *blyókly*—"color" and "withered" (faded). The new adjective is a blend of an old adjective and a noun.

(540) *Kúkol'*—the cuculla (hood) of a Russian Orthodox monk. It has a high pointed top.

(547) *Migolyóty*—a "moment" and a "flight." And plural to boot!

(554) Bely gives the explanation in the footnote, but this might be for some special reason lost to us: one "strange" word is explained by another, even more strange.

(569) Vasíly Ósipovich Klyuchévsky (1841-1911)—Russian historian, professor of Moscow University. A personal friend of Bely's father, professor Nikolay Vasilyevich Bugaev.

(569) Bryusov, Symbolist poet (see line 125).

(569) Dimitry Sergeevich Merezhkovsky (1865-1941)—poet, writer, critic, emigré after the October Revolution. A prominent figure in Russian cultural history of the first half of the twentieth century. Husband of the poet and critic Zinaida Gippius.

(577) Alexander Borisovich Goldenweiser (1875-1961)—virtuoso pianist before the Revolution, professor of the Moscow Conservatory; in 1958 published lively and valuable recollections of Leo Tolstoy.

(579) The "howl" has "grey hair"—or the "greyhaired howl" (of the snow storm)—a synesthesia.

(583) [581] "Sophistries" or "sophistics" (*sofistiki*) is not in Russian, as it is in English, a word meaning something subtle or fallacious (Webster), but it has a derogatory overtone of needless discussion, unnecessarily intricate, beside the point, about a problem that might be resolved in a much simpler way.

(585) *Volódya*—diminutive of Vladimir (Sergeevich Solovyov).

(596) The Russian word is a blend of "black" and "disheveled locks": *chernokósmaya*.

(607) Here again Bely speaks about "atomistic bunk" (or nonsense). At that time, for most people the words "atom" and "atomic" did not so much denote the concrete, tangible physical phenomena as metaphorically imply a most fantastic, mysterious and dazzling (and slightly weird) scientific field.

(608) The "decadents"—as in France at the beginning of the Symbolist movement the term had a derogatory meaning. And as in France during the 1880s, in Russia of the 1890s and even the 1900s the words *dekadénty* and *dekandéntstvo* meant "gibberish," incomprehensible to honest people, weird art and poetry that could shake the established order. The lower middle-class sometimes called the avant-garde *"dekadentísty."* Solovyov (like Chekhov and many others) did not recognize either the fact that these young poets were his devoted followers, or that he himself and the greatest poets of all times were in a way Symbolists, and that after Tolstoy the so-called "realism" of the nineteenth century was coming to its end. By the first years of the new century it became obvious that their protest—a vigorous and eloquent one—was not against a "class," or the oppressive regime, or the stifling political and economic conditions, but

against the dead "academic" tradition, which satisfied primarily the philistines and the bourgeoisie. The enlightened Morozovs, or the Hirshmans, were on the side of the young Symbolists but their own parents—at the universities, in the civil service, in the reactionary press, were *against* them, laughing at them, cursing them as degenerates and "drop-outs," although this generation—with Merezhkovsky, Annensky, Vyacheslav Ivanov, Bryusov, Blok, and Bely—was the most enlightened, European-minded and forward-looking of *all* Russian generations in the whole of Russian history.

(609) "Black mass"; narcotics; strange attire; poets appearing in public with jewelry in their buttonholes (Kuzmin, Severyanin, Viktor Gofman, Khodasevich, and others); women in trousers, barefoot and sitting mostly on the floor; the "odd" way of reciting poetry (not at all in Stanislavsky's Art Theater tradition)—all these helped to build an *eccentric* image of the new generation. In their private and public behavior, the Russian Symbolists were nearer to the English-American Imagists and French Surrealists than to any other literary avant-garde group.

(611) *Kozyól* is a billy goat, and *kozlít'* means "to behave like a billy goat." A strange dance of the period performed in public by a single dancer, uninhibited and wild, was called a *kozlovák*.

(615) These three phenomena obviously disturbed the lofty philosopher. The plague—as one of God's scourges; the Mongols—as the "yellow peril" (his bugaboo for Russia and Europe); and the Ethiopians—as Black Africa.

(617) In the newspapers at the turn of the century there was as much talk about the "erosion of Europe" as there was later about the monster of Loch Ness. However, in Bely's lines there is a second meaning: erosion of the southeast of Europe connected with the Mongolian-Chinese expansion, the "yellow peril."

(624) *Nóvoe Vrémya* was one of the most popular St. Petersburg newspapers during the last decades before the Revolution (began publication in 1868). This was a right-wing daily subsidized by the tsarist government to which, however, some first-rate writers contributed, such as Chekhov and Rozanov. The chief editor (and owner) of the paper was A. S. Suvorin (see Chekhov's correspondence with him in *Anton Chekov's Life and Thought*, trans. S. Karlinsky, M. Heim, Berkeley,

Univ. of California, 1976), who in St. Petersburg also owned a publishing house, a large bookstore, and a theater. In a way he was a counterpart of D. Sytin (1854-1934), the owner (but not the editor) of the big Moscow daily *Rússkoe Slóvo* (which had the largest circulation in Russia, and also closed in 1917). Chekhov's relationship with Suvorin had its parallel in Gorky's connections with Sytin.

(625-26) Demchinsky was not a writer of editorials or international political commentary, but a chatty and free-and-easy journalist, who also regularly predicted the meteorological conditions.

(627) The "atmospheric phenomena" here do not precisely refer to meteorology. This is journalese apparently about some happenings in the "stratosphere," which had superstitious significance for the readers of *Nóvoe Vrémya*.

(634) Magnesium flashes, as in photography.

(636) Agni—see commentary to line 32.

(637) *Zaognít*—Bely's neologism: infinitive would be *zaognít'*. He uses the third person masc. sing. to say: "will become like fire."

(639) [638] *Gromár'*—a neologism coined from the word "thunder" (*grom*) with a typical (masc. sing.) ending. But the "thunder-man" has a second implication: it is also a giant that might break everything around him (*gromít'*). The existing noun derived from *gromít'* is *gromíla*: a housebreaker, thug, hoodlum, ruffian, or mugger.

(640) [641] *Zýbina* is water that shimmers lightly, as derived from *zyb'* ("ripples").

(653) Nicholas, bishop of Myra (Asia Minor), the patron saint of Russia until 1917. Myra was the capital of Lycia, in Russia *Lýka*, thus—*Myr-Lykía*, the place where Saint Nicholas lived, preached, and died in the fourth century. His relics were brought to Bari, Italy, in 1807, and the church where he is buried can be visited.

(654) The Day of the Holy Spirit—see commentary to line 11.

(678) The "forever one" or the "one and only"—always the idea of the eternal feminine, the core of Vladimir Solovyov's philosophy. As in line 336, the words of Solovyov are here repeated: "*Odno, na vek odno*," meaning "the only one for ever" or "the one and only for eternity."

(695-98) Before 1917, in Russian Orthodox cemeteries one could see crypts and inside, through a small window behind an ordinary or sometimes red glass, a tiny icon lamp, an oil lamp *(lampáda)* burning. The same was true in churches, in front of icons. Even in a closed space, the little flame would quiver and flicker (because of the wick floating in oil), giving the impression of either winking, or blinking, or shivering. Here Bely uses personification (one of his beloved tropes) to speak about it.

(698) See commentary to line 502 for the word *vózdukh*. There might have been inside the little chapel some sacred object covered with a brocade napkin, or maybe in this case not a napkin but an embroidered curtain that would move inside the red window, above the icon, or only seem to be moving. It also might be a metaphoric image, a vision of the cross over the chapel and the falling snow drifting over it like a sacred cover.

(701-2) *Begu* . . . Bely was running and rushing from one place to another: from the apartment of Mikhail Solovyov in the neighborhood of Arbat to the cemetery and the grave of Vladimir Solovyov and back again. His way was through Prechístenka (see line 1258), Zúbovsky Boulevard, sometimes cutting through the network of small lanes between Smolénsky Boulevard and Prechístenka, and the "Maiden Field." From there it was one mile to the Novodevíchy Convent.

(704) The unexpected, harsh conclusion with that pedestrian rhyme of *pómer* and *nómer* does not hint at future life and another world. It has here the dryness of a very realistic statement, and the image that is created is not of a "number" of a grave, but a piece of luggage dispatched from somewhere to nowhere.

3.

(707) *Konvért* here means a message, probably the unknown program of the concert. Or more abstractly: going to a concert and not knowing what might happen, something perhaps as relevant as life itself.

(721-23) Eagles, lions, oxen, and bulls—the ancient (and Christian, and anthroposophic) symbols are back. This time there is no internal rhyme as in lines 18-19, but an anaphora four times repeated that gives an unusual intensity to the lines.

(727) Lazulite—see commentary to line 230.

NOTES AND COMMENTS

(729) "Golden-hazel" is blended in one word. *Káry* belongs to a special group of adjectives that pertain only to one single noun, in this case the eyes. See also commentary to line 482.

(730) Heliopolis—Baalbek, ancient city in Lebanon, a Roman colony in the first century A.D., famous for its temple to the sun-god, Baal.

(730) "Maiden Otis" could not be elucidated with certainty: there is Odis, a force of energy emanating from crystals and magnets; there is Otheos, the "most holy name invoked for discovering treasure"; there is *ōtos*, Greek genitive for "ear." All seem inapplicable. The *B. B. Poeta* commentary (generally not very satisfactory) says that this is an "invented" name.

(732) In the text, the word *miozotis* (i.e. myosotis), which is French (and English) for forget-me-not, is used by Bely with the stress on the third (not fourth) syllable. This ironic stress shows that a comic (over sentimental, cute, pretentious, "kitschy") effect was intended.

(733) [735] *Gránnymi*—the horns are not round but faceted. This can be seen in primitive pictures, which show the devil even more frightening because of that distinctive attribute normally seen in goats.

(735) Granite and the color pink are blended in one word.

(736) [733] Apis—see commentary to line 431.

(729-46) There are two symbolic female-figures here: the first, an innocent maiden, a virgin, the object of lewd desires of the sacred bull; the second, a weird image of the embodiment of female lust.

(744) *Zúbrina* (neologism meaning a long, sharp, serrated hard object)—an erotic attribute of the god (Zeus) who comes down from the thundering clouds. In line 115 he was in possession of a trident. The symphonic classical music induced Bely to make "moral" judgments as it did Leo Tolstoy (see his "Kreuter Sonata"). There was a temptation in the sounds, which they both thought to be "sinful."

(746) *Zagréy* is Zagreus, a name which sometimes refers to Zeus, but more often to Dionysus. Divine child of Orphic mythology, he transformed himself to escape the wrath of Hera into a lion, a serpent, a tiger, a bull. But this did not save him, and he was torn apart, and his heart, saved by Athena, was swallowed by Zeus. The name comes apparently from the river Sagra. On Zagreus, Ernst Cassirer wrote in his *Myth of the State*: "Legend of Zagreus is not a mere fairy tale. It has a *fundamentum in*

re: it refers to a certain 'reality.' But this reality is neither physical nor historical; it is *ritual*. What is *seen* in the Dionysic cult is *explained* in the myth."

(748) Grevs—see commentary to line 123.

(749) Vojtĕch Hlaváč, a well-known conductor of Czech origin (1849-1911).

(750) Vasily Il'ich Safonov (1852-1918)—in his youth a virtuoso pianist, later Director of the Moscow Conservatory (after Taneev left in 1889). Conductor of the Moscow Symphony Orchestra. He went abroad, conducted in Vienna, and was invited to the United States. Came to New York as conductor of the New York Philharmonic in 1904, stayed until 1909. At one time Director of the Russian Musical Society.

(752) *"fony"*—plural of the particle "von" denoting a Baltic aristocrat in Imperial Russia, a baron of German origin, usually belonging to the landed gentry and the high tsarist officialdom.

(754) *Ozón* (i.e. ozone) colloquially means pure, fresh air. *Ozonírovat'* (a verb), means "to clean the air" (here, "to clean the breath").

(755) Any kind of musical scale is a *zvukoryád*. Bely here hints at the idea of Rudolf Steiner, who asserted that any harmonious combination of musical sounds supports the universe.

(757-58) The Russian words *bezobrázny* and *bezóbrazny* mean "ugly" and "formless" respectively.

(758) Erebus—a place of darkness where the souls of the dead pass on their way to Hades.

(755-60) Here in five lines Bely gives five different words (notions) derived from one root: the root is *óbraz* ("image"), and the five words are:

    otobrazháet—"reflects" (the universe)
    bezobrázii—"from the ugliness" (of cities)
    bezóbrazy—"to the lack of forms" (of the underworld)
    óbrazov—"to the images" (of men)
    mnogoobráziyami—"by the multiforms" (of skies).

(761) *Vosstónet* means "it will set up a moan," but *vosstánet* means "it will arise." *Pad* comes from *zvezdopád* meaning the falling of stars. There is no sense to the "moaning" indicated here, but the image of the falling

stars rising back again to the skies allows one to presume that an error has been made, and the *o* instead of *a* is a misprint.

(763) The Oreads are nymphs of hills and mountains.

(767) Bely apostrophizes his own verse ironically as Pushkin did. He is even more ironical about it when he calls his verse "simple," and "subdued."

(772) Alekséy Sergéevich Petróvsky—a close friend of Bely through life, especially in the period of "dawn" and World War I. In the memoirs of Bely, Petrovsky appears as a major figure (first volume), and comes across as an alter ego of Bely, his shadow, his follower, and his hanger-on.

(780) Two adjectives *murúgy* and *pégy* are applied only to horses.

(781) *Markóvnikov* was Professor Morkóvnikov, and the spelling is not an error. Bely sometimes showed his disdain for a person by distorting that person's name. "Mademoiselle Stanévich" was called persistently "Mademoiselle Shtanévich" (*shtaný* means pants), no matter how many times one would correct him.

(782) The word here is *burbón* (derived from Bourbon, the name of French kings and dukes), which in Russian means a coarse and rough man.

(782) *Megaera*—a mean old woman, nasty and vile. From this Greek name Bely creates an adjective: *megéraya* (fem.).

(783-85) The onomatopoea (rhyming with "wife of professor"—*proféssorsha*) conveys the rustling of the silk skirts of the ladies. Line 785 is the only one in *Pervoe svidanie* with a pyrrhic on the fourth foot. Such a line is a rarity in Russian poetics: the fourth foot (in a four-foot iambic line) contains the rhyming syllable and therefore has to be stressed. When unstressed it has a playful, ironic effect.

(788) The fashionable boa was a long fur scarf that had at its ends a head of a fox, a sable, or a chinchilla. These heads of dead animals often had a nasty look.

(789) Minangois was one of the fashionable dress designers of Moscow. The other was Lámanova, who had a "salon de couture" until the Revolution.

(791) The new women's fashion came with a wide (ten yards at the

hem), short (showing the ankle), and belted skirt that in French was called *cloche* and in Russian *klyósh*. This was the biggest change in women's fashion to occur in our century before the advent of slacks. In 1918-19, the Soviet "Red Navy" adopted very wide men's trousers, and the sailors wearing them were called *klyóshniki*. There was a ditty at that time:

> Hey vy klyóshniki,
> Da sho vy sdélali?
> Báb'i yúbki na shtaný
> Peredélali!

(800) Countess *Tolstaya* was doubtless the wife of Leo Tolstoy, Sofya Andreevna. She was a friend of S. I. Tanéev (see commentary below to line 854), who—as the gossip went—was in love with her. Tolstoy (in 1887-89) vented his jealousy by writing the "Kreutzer Sonata." *Tólsty* means "fat." Sofya Andreevna of course was fat, as were most of the middle-aged ladies of that period. The pun is untranslatable.

(811) *Doldónit bében' barabána* is onomatopoeic and conveys the beating of the kettle drums.

(821) *Zarnéy* is Bely's neologism. It is the comparative form of a nonexistent adjective. There is no word *zarnóy* (derived from *zaryá*), and therefore one might presume that this is a rare case (if not the only one) when an adjective has been formed in its comparative degree without having a positive one.

(821) The Russian word *neopalímey* is used also in lines 1300-11 when Bely speaks about the Neopalímov Lane, where the little church of the "Virgin of the Burning Bush," with its icon, is standing. The word here (an adjective) is used in its comparative form.

(820-23) These lines tell us about the first appearance of Zariná. This is one of the climaxes of the poem, but not the main one. Here she arrives and is escorted by her husband into the concert hall and passes by Bely and others. The grand moment comes in lines 1080-83 when she departs from the Hall of Nobles.

(826) Emanuel Swedenborg (1688-1772)—for the first part of his life, he was a scientist, philosopher, and writer. After 1743, he started to have visions and went into spiritual research and interpretation of the Scrip-

tures. His followers formed a sect not only in Sweden (his country of origin), but also around the world. It was called The New Jerusalem.

(830) *Bryzn'*—a neologism formed from the verb *brýzgat'* ("splash" or "spray"); here it is a noun used only in plural; *brýzgi*.

(835) Melanite—see commentary to line 231.

(837) *Véernye rechi* is an ambiguity and might have two meanings: first it can refer to the "fan language" used by the ladies at the concert, moving their beautiful fans in a certain elaborate way. Second, the speech of the ladies, equivocal, coquettish, evasive, was as playful as the movements of a fan.

(839) As in line 50 and later in line 1021, there is here, if not a light parody on Pushkin, at least a reminiscence of *Eugene Onegin*. See "Al'bóm Onégina," stanza 9, lines 9-10, as a rule printed among addenda to the novel, or as "fragments." (These lines 838-39 are repeated at the end of the poem, lines 1090-91.)

(840-41) Ghibelline and Guelf are, respectively, a member of the aristocratic party in medieval Italy, and a member of the papal party, opposed to the authority of the German emperors. The play of words is *gíbly—gibellín*, which means "doomed Ghibelline."

(842) The Russian word *potéshny* has two meanings: the first is "amusing," the second is the name of a regiment created to amuse the young Tsar Peter the Great. Here both meanings are blended: Bely says he is an amusing Knight of his Lady. The Alkonost edition has a misprint: *paladín* should have one *l*.

(847) *Báben'* is a derogatory word applied to a man; it means "looking like an old fat woman," some sort of a eunuch (not to be confused with *bábnik*, also offensive, meaning "skirt chaser").

(849) The poem by Alexander Blok is from the *Poems of the Beautiful Lady*, part 9, line 1902. The first stanza reads:

> I am the adolescent who lights the candles,
> And keeps the censor burning.
> She with no thought and no word
> Laughs from the other shore.

As very often happened, Bely made an error in his quotation (in the third line).

NOTES AND COMMENTS

(854) Sergéy Ivánovich Tanéev (1856-1915)—composer, pianist, conductor. Friend of Tchaikovsky, Rachmaninov, Leo Tolstoy, and others. He composed the opera *Oresteia*.

(855) [856] The noun "binoculars" has served here to form a verb: to observe through binoculars: *binóklit'*.

(856) [855] Dimitri Fyodorovich Trepov (1855-1906)—the son of F. F. Trepov, who was the target of Vera Zasulich's assassination, one of the notorious revolutionary acts of the nineteenth century. The other son, Alexander (1862-1928), was the minister of public transportation in 1915, and in 1916 the chairman of the Council of Ministers, which was one of the last attempts of the tsar to save the monarchy. Dimitri, after serving as chief of police in Moscow (1896-1905), became the Governor-General of St. Petersburg (1905-6), where he was responsible for the "Bloody Sunday" (January 9, 1905) shooting into the crowd of unarmed demonstrators. Bely made a mistake in Trepov's initial.

(871) Norns—the three goddesses of Fate in Scandinavian epic.

(872) The raven of Wotan (or Woden, or Odin)—the chief god of Norse mythology, and the raven—his main symbol. Both images (as well as the Norns) appear in Wagner's *Götterdämmerung*.

(882) Ivan Grzhimali (1844-1915), concertmaster of the Moscow Symphony.

(883) A neologism ingeniously built from "violin" and "musician"—*skrípka* and *muzykánty*.

(884) *Kalách* is a large loaf of twisted and braided wheat bread. It is meant to be eaten by one person. To draw apart one's knees and twist one's feet, in the shape of a *kalách* is a common expression. Another is to sleep *kaláchikom* (diminutive of *kalach*)—in the fetal position.

(885) *Prápor* is slang, a derogatory name for a *práporshchik* (approximately an ensign or junior lieutenant).

(886) The French expression "ce qu'on appelle" is here shortened and vulgarized to sound like *skonapel*. Unlike French, English words are not easily made "funny" in Russian: neither "spleen," nor "lady," nor "week-end," nor "cocktail" have any elements that can be distorted in a ridiculous way. (The first two were incorporated 150 years ago, the last two entered the Russian language with 4,800 other words of British and American origin after 1967 with the blessings of the Academy of Sciences

of the USSR.) But French expressions are easy prey for parody, and so are German.

(891) Morózov, the husband of Zariná. See commentary on line 36.

(902) Alexander Nikolaevich Scriábin (1872-1915)—the famous Russian composer.

(918) The correct accent (stress) in the word *zadokhnyótsya* would be on the third syllable. Bely takes license by putting the stress on the second syllable and gets away with it.

(932) *Pukh* and *peró* ("down" and "feather")—Bely makes one word out of two: blending them in an adjective.

(933) The Alkonost edition has a misprint in the possessive pronoun.

(934) Literally: a "mousy colt," an idiomatic expression meaning a frisky elderly man who tries to look and behave younger than he is. Like the image of the *prápor* (line 885), both are symbols of triviality.

(943) The Russian word *mnogoyáky* ("having many aspects") was coined by Bely with the example of *dvoyáky* and *troyáky* in mind. The misprint in the Slovo edition has been corrected in the *B. B. Poeta*.

(944) The ending *iy* of one-syllable nouns in the nominative case (in Cyrillic ИЙ) is always masculine, can never be anything else, and in such words as *zmiy* (a serpent), *kiy* (a billiard cue), *Viy* (a horror figure in Gogol's tale) are the very symbols of masculinity. To this group belongs the three-letter Russian word for the male organ. The words of two syllables ending with Й —*geróy* ("hero"), *kholúy* ("groveller," "flunky")—follow suit, and have the same connotation.

(954-62) There are thirty-four sibilants in nine lines: s, zh, sh, s, zh, shch, sh, ch, z, sh, s, sh, s, s, zh, s, sh, s, s, ch, sh, sh, ch, s, sh, sh, sh, sh, sh, sh, sh, sh, s.

(960-61) *Klikúsha* means any hysterical woman (colloquial), one who cries and sobs loudly and publicly.

(964) She (capitalized: *Ona*) is Zarina, the Madonna, and also the French horn, which in Russian is feminine (*valtórna*). The beauty of the sound of the horn in the symphony orchestra (under the baton of Safonov) was already evoked in lines 875-76. The synesthesia here is the sound of the French horn and Raphael's Madonna, which combine to produce the image of Margarita Morózova, Bely's first love, and it sig-

121

nals the approaching climax of the "first encounter" that started to build up in lines 820-23.

(964) There is a misprint in "Slovo": not *ozernéy* but *ozornéy*.

(968) [967] *Viegolóvy* (a five-syllable word)—a creature having the head of *Viy* (Gogol's evil spirit, an image of horror).

(967-76) These lines give us one synesthesia after another, and the sound-play is so dense that the meaning of the words on their denotative and logical level can hardly be grasped without pausing and rereading. This is a case when, as T. S. Eliot said, we enjoy poetry before we understand what it is about—merely by hearing the sounds and accepting it as babbling. This is not the "nonsense" verse, or "transsense" that was practiced by such poets as Khlebnikov. This is poetry at its highest level. The musical and pictorial elements are blended, and we have (as in certain poems of Bely, or even in certain paragraphs of his prose) the feeling of his incontestable greatness. In lines 967-76, nine lines out of ten contain "unorthodox" rhythmic variations and only one traditional four-foot iambic line; they give us six different rhythmic patterns (out of the seven that exist). This is one of the highest points that Bely attained in his creative handling and use of words. In this he was the first, the greatest, and perhaps the only one who realized fully the absolute value, the pathos, the irony, the synesthetic (and aesthetic) possibilities of the Russian word. Never before or after Bely was there such a release of the hidden and neglected creative forces of the Russian language as he liberated here. This gave a new dimension to the basic material that poetry is made of, and to the craft of the poet as well, which is brought to a climax in the complete freedom of his vision and his use of sound.

(977) Mary and Martha from the Gospels, two symbols of the eternal Feminine, one celestial, the other earthly.

(980) The Alkonost edition has a misprint: not *raey* but *vest'u*.

(983-86) Bely continues his parallels between symbols of the Eternal Feminine with the three sisters and their mother Sophia, whose name means "Wisdom" in Greek.

(987-88) The inversion here is extremely involved, probably more involved than any in the poetry of Vyacheslav Ivanov, who made his inversions often seem unwarranted when neither the rhyming nor the meter required them, apparently merely for the sake of making it harder to read and comprehend, and to give himself the pleasure of creating a new and strange-sounding order of words. The inversions of Bely are far from that, but this one is unusually intricate, even on the border of clumsiness. Putting the words in their logical sequence yields: *soedinív glubinóy chetýre síly v troyákoy býli* ("uniting by their depth four forces in their threefold reality"), where *býli* is a noun in its singular form (fem., locative) and means "in their (threefold) reality."

(990)   The Only One—is an image of the eternal feminine.

(995-1002)   This is a repetition of an earlier image. The misprint in the Slovo edition has been rectified in the *B. B. Poeta: lazúli*.

(1000)   *Vozdukholyótny*, a noun ("air") and a verb ("fly") have been blended in one adjective and applied to the musical term *septakórd* ("a seventh").

(1012)   Bely's footnote to this line is misleading: the correct line of Lermontov's from his poem *"Kak chásto pyóstroyu tolpóyu okruzhón"* (1840) is:

> I love the vision evoked by my day-dream
> *With her eyes filled by azure fire,*
> With her smile as rosy as the first beam
> Of a new day over the distant grove.

But the line of Solovyov says *"ochámi"*, not *"glazámi"*:

> In the midst of a crimson light,
> *With eyes filled with azure fire,*
> You were looking around, as if you were
> The first radiance of a universal and creative day.
>
>   (XCVII, 1915 edition)

Here Solovyov used for "eyes" the Old Church Slavonic synonym. In addition to the "azure" in this line, there are three more times that Solovyov speaks in the same poem about the sky-blue color: (a) "The azure is around me, it is in my heart"; (b) "She was pierced by golden azure"; and (c) "All of a sudden everything is filled with golden azure." This gave Bely the title of his first volume of verse, *Gold in Azure* (*Zoloto v lazuri*, Moscow, Skorpion, 1904).

(1019)   Once more the intonation and the sound (and the rhythm) remind one of Pushkin's verse (Tatiana's letter in *Eugene Onegin*).

NOTES AND COMMENTS

(1022) [1021] *Ogolubít'*—the verb is in infinitive form and created from the adjective *golubóy* ("light-blue"): to make blue. If the accent is switched to the second syllable the verb means "to caresse": *golúbit'*.

(1027) *Opurpúr'*—to make purple; a verb made of the adjective *purpúrny*, and used here in the imperative.

(1038) The light of Saint Elmo (or Saint Elmo's fire)—an electrical phenomenon sometimes observed in stormy weather on a ship, such as on the mast or in rigging. Saint Elmo is the patron saint of sailors.

(1039) Damascus—the road to Damascus, where Saul saw the Light.

(1046) *Migolyóty*—see commentary to line 547.

(1065) The image here is daring and beautiful: Safonov with his baton sailing in the clouds over our planet, and now heading home "to Moscow," short, fat, sweating, and happy. See lines 115-18: the old professors, short, fat, and happy descending from the clouds to make love to their wives.

(1080-83) This is the high point of the poem, prepared for by lines 820-23 and 964. Not "She will pass," but "She passes." And as it was *zarnéy*, now it is *zarnímey*, i.e. the first time a comparative adjective formed from (nonexisting) *zarnóy*, the second time a comparative adjective formed from (nonexisting) *zarnímy*. In lines 820-23, the rhythm was not very original

```
- /    - /    - -    - /
- /    - /    - -    - / -
- /    - /    - -    - /
- -    - /    - -    - / -
```

Now the rhythm goes

```
- -    - /    - /    - / -
- -    - /    - -    - /
- /    - /    - -    - / -
- /    - /    - -    - /
```

and instead of Zarina being illuminated by the lights of the concert hall, she is illuminated by herself, and apparently illuminating everything around her. Instead of her having a name (that is "in-her-name") she now "wears" her *in Nomine* as if it were the train of her gown.

(1103) Vladimir Vladimirovich Kallásh (1866-1918)—the editor of Gogol's *Complete Works and Correspondence* (1907-9) in nine volumes. Galosh in Russian is *kalósha*.

(1105) Ivan Alekseevich Kablukóv (1857-1942)—professor of chemistry at Moscow University. Bely attended his lectures. The heel of a shoe in Russian is *kablúk*.

(1107) Nos is not only the name of a Moscow lawyer, but is also *nos* ("nose") and the title of Gogol's tale. Vladimir Ivanovich Shenrók (1853-1910) was the author of one of the first compilations of bio-bibliographical material on Gogol'. Here "The Nose" was in attendance but alone, without his friend Mr. Shenrok.

4.

(1113) The bonfires were braziers that the coachmen lit on street corners while awaiting their patrons and masters when the winter temperatures in Moscow fell below freezing.

(1118) *Gíknut'* or *progigíknut'*—the verb *gíkat'* ("gee-up") in its perfective aspect with a strong onomatopoeic effect.

(1119-20) The voice of the coachman is reflected by the falling snow. This could be called a "synesthetic catachresis," i.e. a mixture of sound and visual image that verges on the illogical or even on the absurd.

(1130) *Snegoverchénye*—the whirlpools of the blizzard forming in the air; blend of two nouns: "snow" and the action of circling. (*Stoloverchénye* means spiritualistic table-turning.)

(1131) *Svetomolénie*—synesthesia with "light" and "prayers" in one neologism.

(1136) The right word for "spending time at dusk" is *súmernichat'*. Bely makes his own word with a slightly different meaning: "passing through dusk and somehow coloring the objects [here, the houses] in grey" (implying space and movement).

(1140) "*Stróit' túry*" comes from the French and is a recurrent expression in Bely's poetry—see his "Maskarad." The meaning of the words is not only "making some intricate ballet steps around someone," but also doing it mischievously (compare: *stróit' rózhi* and *stróit' kúry*).

(1143) The Doppelgänger who walks along on four legs is the shadow of the poet.

(1144) *Zvezdenéet*—a verb made from the noun *zvezdá* ("star"). The spirit is not fourlegged: it has two wings and is as bright as a star. The sound *z* (lines 1144-49) is here predominant.

(1146-53) There is an erotic image here that Bely did not develop. The hint of an erection is obvious but perhaps should not be pinpointed. Something happens to him mysteriously among "lilies" (innocence?), and the word "sinful" shows his Victorianism (he would not deny it). The whole passage is blurred by an overwhelming emotionality, which, as Mahler once said (quoted by Bulez): "expressed hyperbolically, destroys the unity of the form, impairs the harmony between it and the subject-matter. The relationship between the idea and its expression are drowned in the all overflowing unbridled manifestation that lost control of itself."

(1170) *Ya—omólnen*, from *mólniya* ("lightning"): "possessed by lightning" or "bristling with lightning."

(1189) *Pustovorót* and *pustoplyás*—playful and whimsical words formed with the adjective *pustóy* ("empty"); the words "turning around" and "prancing" or "jumping" in a mad way. In line 1223 the word *pustovoróty* (this time in plural) is used in a coined expression: *pustovoróty bytiyá*—"the empty whirlpools of existence."

(1202) The word *perevoprósim* is a neologism: again and again we will "ask," "inquire," "put questions" (excessively).

(1205) *Brémenno* should not be confused with *berémenno*, which means "pregnant." The meaning here is "heavy," "burdensome," "weighing heavily upon the earth."

(1217) The word "chaos" in Russian might be pronounced in two ways: *kháos* with the stress on the first syllable, which is the correct way, and *khavós* (slang) with the stress on the second, and a *v* in the middle. The difference can be approximated in English by the words "potatoes" and "taters."

(1220-21) The sound pattern in these two lines that speak of "our common future" is:

NOTES AND COMMENTS

$$- - - \, , - - - \quad \, , -$$
Peretopatyvaem v gody
$$- \, - - \, , - - - \quad \quad ,$$
I—utopatyvaem r tmy

where we can hear the fast running of feet.

(1227) *Potópnye godá* might have two meanings: first, the years of the Flood, of "my" deluge (of personal catastrophe); second, the years of something that happened "to me" so very long ago: *dopotópny*—"antediluvian."

(1232) There is a miscalculation here. The iambic line that should have nine syllables has ten, which seems an error made by Bely himself. It certainly is not a misprint; it could be changed easily by using either "*Otkrovéniem Iánna*" or "*Otkrovén'em Ioánna*" (both [¯] ¯ ¯ ′ ¯ ¯ ¯ ′ ¯). Both would be perfect, containing eight syllables (plus one). This was repeated in all three editions and certainly was not noticed by anyone.

(1238-45) Again Bely is playing with anachronisms, reminding one of Pushkin in *Eugene Onegin*, Chapter VIII, stanza 1.

(1250) There is an impression now that the end of the poem is near, that one combined word (noun plus verb = adjective, or noun plus adjective = adjective, or verb, etc.) brings about another, forming a crescendo. Here we have *belopokróvy*—an adjective and a noun forming a new noun in the plural.

(1250) *Vetroplyásy* immediately follows two nouns together forming a third in the plural: "dances of the winds."

(1251) The model of *svetélitsa* is *metélitsa*—the first noun comes from "light" and the second from "blizzard"; and *svetélitsa* is preceded by a gerund from a related verb (*metyás'*).

(1253) Savior is *Spasítel'*; there also exists the shortened form *Spas*. It is a more intimate, perhaps the most intimate and endearing form, of address in speaking to the Lord.

(1258) *Prechístenka* comes as a refrain—the street running from the Southwest corner of Moscow down to the convent, the cemetery, the clinics, the "Maiden Field." With Arbát this was at that time the center of the Moscow intellectual community, who lived there mostly in their small (e.g. Gershenzon) and not so small (e.g. Tolstoy) wooden houses.

(1269) The lack of a question mark in the Alkonost edition is a misprint.

(1275) The sound is striking: *kúbovovovóy*.

(1286-87) The "Maiden Field," where he arrives, after running along *Prechístenka* away from the center of the city.

(1289) Running all the way to the convent through a snowstorm seems too strenuous, so he hails a horse-drawn sleigh.

(1293) As in the "Bronze Horseman" (Pushkin) and in the "Overcoat" (Gogol'), which are set in St. Petersburg, so in Moscow there are also ghosts in the streets. And here appears the giant figure of the philosopher Vladimir Solovyov, but only for a moment. The rhyme *géyser—Goldenwéiser* is repeated. And we come to the end of this night journey.

(1300-11) There is a small church looking like a chapel in Neopalímov Lane. The name is given to the lane in honor of the little church. The church was built to commemorate the Burning Bush more specifically (Exod. 3:2-5), in honor of an icon, *Virgin of the Burning Bush*. This icon guards the people of Russia from fire. They pray here to the Virgin to safeguard them and their wooden houses from the distress and misery of fire. Is there an association with Agni, or is it only a coincidence? Neopalímov Lane (*pereúlok*) has a special sound: in both words there are two vowels side by side, which is always a welcome relief in Russian speech. The Russian language—and this is common knowledge—has clusters of consonants that sometimes are difficult to pronounce, and rather unattractive when emphasized. Whenever there is a combination of two vowels next to each other, this gives beauty to the speech, relief from the clusters of consonants, and melody to the phrase. These two vowels must always be pronounced separately, not crumpled as a diphthong; they should be distinctly heard. The two months of summer are *iyún'* and *iyúl'*; it has to be made certain that both words have two syllables each, and not one.

The image of the Burning Bush was the subject of a poem of Vladimir Solovyov:

> In front of me a bush of blackthorn
> Was ablaze with fire but was not consumed.
> (xxxii, 1915 edition)

And Blok referred to the Burning Bush in his famous line "*Déva, Zaryá, Kupiná*" (vol. I, April 4, 1902): "Maiden, Sun-rise, Burning Bush" (fem. and Church-Slavonic).

(1311)   The poem ends with a synechdoche in which the Mother of God looks in front of her, not with her "tearful eye," but with her "thoughtful teardrop."

EPILOGUE

(1312)   The twenty years are the years 1901-21, from the year Bely was 21 to the year when he was 41.

(1315)   He repeats the expression: the Day of the Holy Spirit, from line 11.

(1319)   In the last line Bely uses an oxymoron: "the never reposing silence" (never abating peace, never hushing quiet).

APPENDIX I

Repeated Passages by Line Numbers in Russian Text

Part 1:

a. 49; 131; 221
b. 57-60; 242-45

Pattern: a-b-a′-a″-b′

Part 2:

c. 268-69; 563-64
d. 273-80; 696-702
e. 283-84; 644-45
f. 288-90; 417-19
g. 299-302; 412-15; 685-88
h. 335-42; 677-84
i. 343; 480

Pattern: c-d-e-f-g-h-i-g′-f′-i′-c′-e′-h′-g″-d′

Part 3:

j. 730-36; 995-1002
k. 802-5; 1095-97
l. 820-27; 984-86; 1080-87
m. 832-35; 1003-6
n. 836-39; 1088-91
o. 843; 876
p. 850-52; 1072-75
q. 861-63; 910-12
r. 881-83; 1059-61
s. 889-93; 1076-79

APPENDIX I

From Part 2:
A. 1046-48 (547-48)
B. 1092-94 (409-11)

Pattern: j-k-l-m-n-o-p-q-o′-r-s-q′-l′-j′-m′-A-r′-p′-s′-l″-n′-B-k′

Part 4:

From Part 3:
C. 1210 (952)
D. 1238-45 (1019-27)
t.   1256-57; 1310-11
u.   1258-61; 1282-85

From Part 2:
E. 1265 (672)
F. 1266-72 (579-85 and 673-76 combined)
G. 1278-81 (634-37)
H. 1296-99 (575-78)

Pattern: C-D-t-u-E-F-G-u′-H-t′

APPENDIX II

TABLE 1

Stress Apportionment (by percentage)

Syllable	2	4	6	8
Parts 1-2	74.8	88.0	36.6	100
Parts 3-4	70.9	91.2	33.0	99.8
Pushkin	85.5	96.4	40.7	100

SOURCE: Adapted from Taranovsky, op. cit., p. 129.

TABLE 2

Rhythmic Variations (by percentage)

Types	I	II	III	IV	V	VI	Remainder
Parts 1-2	16.4	8.5	11.7	46.5	0.3	16.6	—
Parts 3-4	17.4	7.0	8.5	44.7	0.2	22.1	0.2
Pushkin	32.2	6.3	3.4	49.7	0.2	9.4	—

SOURCE: Adapted from Taranovsky, op. cit., p. 130.

LIBRARY OF CONGRESS CATALOGING IN PUBLICATION DATA

Bugaev, Boris Nikolaevich, 1880-1934.
  The first encounter.

  Translation of Pervoe svidanie.
  Parallel text of the poem in English and Russian.
  I. Janeček, Gerald J. II. Berberova, Nina Nikolaevna
III. Title.
PG3453.B84P413   1979   891.7'1'42   78-70276
ISBN 0-691-06381-8

Printed by Libri Plureos GmbH in Hamburg, Germany